An Instant Guide to
MEDICINAL
PLANTS

*The medicinal plants of North America
and their uses described and
illustrated in full color*

PAMELA FOREY AND RUTH LINDSAY

GRAMERCY BOOKS
NEW YORK

Warning Symbol

 Throughout the book this sign has been used to indicate either that caution is needed in the use of this plant or parts of it or that it may be mistaken for other plants which are poisonous and needs special care in identification.

The reader is advised never to experiment and to consult an expert if in any doubt.

Distribution Map

● Commonly found in these areas

○ Present but less common or reaching the limits of its distribution

Copyright © 1991 by Atlantis Publications Ltd.
All rights reserved under International and Pan-American
Copyright Conventions.
No part of this book may be reproduced or transmitted in any form or by any
means electronic or mechanical including photocopying, recording, or by
any information storage and retrieval system, without permission in writing
from the publisher.
This 1999 edition is published by Gramercy Books™
an imprint of Random House Value Publishing, Inc.,
201 East 50th Street, New York, New York 10022.
Gramercy Books™ and colophon are trademarks of
Random House Value Publishing, Inc.
Random House
New York • Toronto • London • Sydney • Auckland
http://www.randomhouse.com/
Printed in Singapore
Library of Congress Cataloging-in-Publication Data
Forey, Pamela.
    An instant guide to medicinal plants : the medicinal plants of
North America and their uses described and illustrated in full color
/ Pamela Forey and Ruth Lindsay.
        p.   cm.
    Originally published : New York : Crescent Books, 1991.
    Includes index.
    ISBN 0-517-69113-2
    1. Medicinal plants—North America—Handbooks, manuals, etc.
2. Materia medica, Vegetable—North America—Handbooks, manuals,
etc. I. Lindsay, Ruth. II. Title.
RM171.F67   1999
615'.32'097—dc21   98-29076
                                                         CIP

14 13 12 11 10

Contents

Introduction

Men have used plants for their medical properties since before records began. However since the advent of modern medicine and modern drugs, many herbal remedies have fallen into disuse. Some modern drugs, like morphine and digitalin, are still obtained from plants, and many herbs provide gentle and effective ways of maintaining the health of the body without recourse to artificial chemicals. Plants contain essential oils, vitamins, alkaloids and glycosides, mucilage and tannins, all natural chemicals which affect the body. Some are important drugs, others stimulate digestion or kidney function, others are antiseptic or aid healing etc.

Plants which are going to be used for herb medicine can be grown in the garden, collected from the wild or obtained from a herbalist. Probably the easiest and safest way of obtaining medicinal herbs is to grow them in the garden, for then you can be certain of their identification and sure they are not contaminated with pesticides. Accurate identification of plants is essential in herb medicine for several reasons. Each species of plant contains specific natural chemicals and therefore each affects the body differently. Some harmless plants used in herb medicine resemble poisonous plants, for example Caraway and Parsley, which are both used in herb medicine, resemble Poison Hemlock which is very poisonous. For this reason it is safer not to collect any wild plant unless you are absolutely certain of its identity.

The best time to pick plants which are going to be used in herbal medicine is in the early afternoon, on a dry sunny day and they should be transported in a basket, not a polythene bag. Picking them in the morning when they are still wet with dew or on a wet day is not a good idea. This is because the active ingredients of the plants are at their highest in the sunlight and because most plants are dried for use in herbal medicine. If they are damp to start with they are more likely to become mouldy before they are properly dried. Stems and leaves or flower stems may be bound into bunches and hung up to dry, alternatively they may be broken up while still fresh, spread out and left to dry in an airy place. Roots should be washed and brushed clean, dried and chopped; the pieces can then be spread out to dry thoroughly. The dried fragmented herbs can be stored in glass jars.

In the home, herbs are most commonly used as infusions, decoctions, as washes or compresses, or in baths. Tea is the most common infusion, it is made when dried leaves of tea are steeped in boiling water. A decoction is made when the dried herb is brought to the boil in water and then soaked in the water for several minutes; the resulting liquid is then used. A wash may be an infusion or decoction; the liquid is used to bathe the skin of the affected part or it can be added to a bath. A bath may be full size, or it may be big enough for a foot bath, eye bath etc. If the liquid is used to soak a piece of gauze which is then bound over, an inflamed joint for example, then this is a herbal compress.

How to use this book

The book is divided into eight sections, depending on which part of the plant is used in herbal medicine. The sections are **Whole Plants**; **Roots and Rhizomes**; **Leaves and Shoots**; **Flowers**; **Fruits and Seeds**; **Bark**; **Multi-use Plants**; **Other Useful Plants**. In addition there are two other sections at the end of the book, **Dangerous Plants** and **Poisonous Plants**. The first of these sections includes plants that need special care in their usage and the second section includes plants that are used in modern medicine, but which are too dangerous to use in the home. Each section is identified by a different color band at the top of the page. Some plants have more than one active part; so a plant may have active leaves and roots. Where one part is more important in herb medicine than the other, then the plant is included in the section of its most important part. Where, for example, fruits and leaves are equally important the plants have been included in the section on multi-use plants. If you want to find a plant for a particular medicinal purpose, then you should turn to the Medical Glossary on pages 11–13.

What's on a page

In the main part of the book, a single species is described on each page. A few pages contain details of an additional related species that is also used in herb medicine. There are four boxes of information on each page. The characteristic features of the plant are described in the first box, its habitat and distribution in the second, its uses in herb medicine in the third and the parts used together with any similar or related medicinal species in the fourth.

Characteristics of your plant

Plants can rarely be identified by a single feature. It is usually the combination of flower type, flower arrangement, leaf shape and leaf arrangement that tells you this is the right one. The information in the first box together with the illustration will help you to identify the plant. Accurate identification is essential; if you are in any doubt, do not use the plant, for some species are deadly poisonous.

Habitat and distribution

The area and habitat in which a species is found often provides important clues to its identity. The distribution map (see page 6) will enable you to see at a glance whether the plant occurs in your part of North America. The second box on each page provides information about its habitat and distribution; a species may not be present throughout its whole range but will be restricted to suitable habitats.

The Plant in Herbal Medicine

In the third box details are given of the medical properties of the plant and its uses. A cross reference has been provided in the Medical Glossary to enable you to find plants for particular uses. The part of the plant which is used is given in the fourth box.

In addition a warning sign in the illustrations of some of the plants 💀 has been used to indicate that care is needed in their use, either because too strong a dose can cause unpleasant symptoms, or because they can be mistaken for poisonous plants. The use of this symbol is in addition to the sections on Dangerous and Poisonous Plants at the end of the book.

Specimen Page

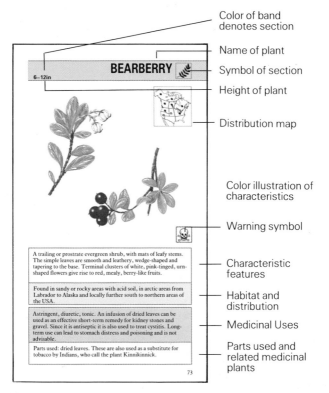

Color of band denotes section

Name of plant

BEARBERRY

6–12in

Symbol of section

Height of plant

Distribution map

Color illustration of characteristics

Warning symbol

A trailing or prostrate evergreen shrub, with mats of leafy stems. The simple leaves are smooth and leathery, wedge-shaped and tapering to the base. Terminal clusters of white, pink-tinged, urn-shaped flowers give rise to red, mealy, berry-like fruits.

Characteristic features

Found in sandy or rocky areas with acid soil, in arctic areas from Labrador to Alaska and locally further south to northern areas of the USA.

Habitat and distribution

Astringent, diuretic, tonic. An infusion of dried leaves can be used as an effective short-term remedy for kidney stones and gravel. Since it is antiseptic it is also used to treat cystitis. Long-term use can lead to stomach distress and poisoning and is not advisable.

Medicinal Uses

Parts used: dried leaves. These are also used as a substitute for tobacco by Indians, who call the plant Kinnikinnick.

Parts used and related medicinal plants

73

Similar useful plants

In the fourth box related medicinal herbs are described. Their medicinal uses may be similar or quite different. Also, warnings are included here about similar or related poisonous plants that may be mistaken for the featured plant.

Other Useful Species

At the end of the book there are six pages of *Other Useful Species*. Included here are plants which have less important uses in herbal medicine than the featured species, either because they have less potent active ingredients or because they have fewer uses, etc.

Dangerous Plants ☠

Some plants that are highly effective herbal remedies, like **Goldenseal** and **Butterfly Weed**, have to be used with care, for they have unpleasant effects or are poisonous in large doses. They have been included in this special section towards the back of the book. Pay particular attention also to those plants with **Warning** symbols in the main part of the book, which also need to be used or identified carefully.

Poisonous plants ☠

There are some plants used in herbal medicine that are impossible to exclude from any book on medicinal plants, but which cannot be recommended for use in the home. Plants like **Foxglove** and **Henbane** have been known for their medicinal effects for centuries but their active ingredients are extremely potent, and poisonous even in small doses. We have included some such plants in a special section of Poisonous Plants that are also used in medicine. We have not included here poisonous plants that are not used in medicine.

Medical Glossary

The following terms and phrases are all used in the text. They indicate the uses to which plants can be put in herbal medicine. Plants which have these properties are also included here so that you can refer directly to them.

Anti-inflammatory Controls inflammation, when the body reacts to infection or injury by reddening, swelling and pain in the affected region. Agrimony, Blackcurrant, Willow, Oak, Marsh Mallow, Coltsfoot.

Antiseptic Destroys bacteria that cause infection. Coneflower, Marjoram, Garlic, Birthroot, Peppermint, Pine, Bearberry, Juniper, Sweet Gum, Sumac.

Antispasmodic Relieves muscle spasms and cramps. Silverweed,

11

Celandine, Agrimony, Catnip, Motherwort, Yarrow, Valerian, Balm, Wild Yam, New Jersey Tea, Peppermint, Gumplant, St John's Wort, Fennel, Caraway, Coriander.

Astringent Draws tissues together and dries up secretions of the body. Useful to stop bleeding and diarrhea and to relieve piles (hemorrhoids.) Butter and Eggs, Silverweed, Plantain, Knotweed, Agrimony, Lady's Mantle, Vervain, Eyebright, Ground Ivy, Yarrow, Sweet Goldenrod, Horseweed, Purple Loosestrife, Water Avens, Cranesbill, Horsetail, Birthroot, Sheep Sorrel, Strawberry, Bearberry, Pipsissewa, Woolly Mullein, Hawthorn, Dogwood, Black Cherry, Witch Hazel, Sweet Gum, Sumac, Apple, Willow, Oak, Horse Chestnut, Birch, Blackberry, Raspberry.

Carminative Dispels wind from the stomach and intestines. Yellow Sweet Clover, Marjoram, Catnip, Carrot, Angelica, Sweet Flag, Colicroot, Balm, Peppermint, Fennel, Caraway, Parsley, Juniper.

Demulcent Soothes inflammation. Plantain, Polypody, American Ginseng, Flax, Woolly Mullein, Marsh Mallow, Slippery Elm.

Digestive Improves digestion. Celandine, Water Avens, Chicory, Sweet Flag, St John's Wort, Fennel, Caraway, Mustard, Juniper, Barberry, Parsley, Dandelion.

Diuretic Increases the flow of urine, aiding the body expel excess water. Butter and Eggs, Cleavers, Knotweed, Horsemint, Sweet Goldenrod, Carrot, Horseradish, Horsetail, Wild Yam, Sheep Sorrel, Watercress, Bearberry, Pipsissewa, Blackcurrant, Hops, Apple, Juniper, Parsley, Dandelion, Hawthorn, Elder, Birch.

Emetic Causes vomiting. Mustard, Elder.

Emollient Softens and soothes (the skin for example.) Yellow Sweet Clover, Woolly Mullein, Flax, Marsh Mallow, Slippery Elm, Basswood.

Expectorant Promotes expulsion of phlegm from the chest, relieving bronchial coughs. Plantain, Violet, Marjoram, Horehound, Polypody, Angelica, Garlic, Coltsfoot, Watercress, Holly, Pine, Gumplant, Woolly Mullein, St John's Wort, Fennel, Horse Chestnut.

Kills worms Polypody, Garlic, Wild Senna.

Laxative Relieves constipation. Boneset, Violet, Polypody, Wild Senna, Mustard, Flax, Apple, Barberry, Cascara Sagrada, Elder.

Promotes bile flow from the liver, hence stimulates the liver and aids digestion Celandine, Chicory, Agrimony, Dandelion.

Promotes milk flow in nursing mothers Vervain, Stinging Nettle, Fennel.

Promotes sweating Catnip, Yarrow, Garlic, Balm, Wild Sarsaparilla, Elder.

Purgative A strong laxative. Butter and Eggs, Celandine, Polypody, Elder.

Purifies the blood Coneflower, Apple.

Reduces fever Boneset, Sheep Sorrel, Strawberry, Balm, Holly, Willow, Horse Chestnut, Dogwood.

Relieves pain Peppermint, Wintergreen, Hops, Prickly Ash, Willow.

Rubefacient Causes reddening and blistering. Horseradish, Pine, Juniper.

Sedative Soothing, reduces restlessness, may induce sleep. Balm, Marjoram, Motherwort, St John's Wort, Hops, Hawthorn, Black Cherry.

Soothes nerves Valerian, Hops.

Stimulant Speeds up the metabolism of the body. Horseradish, Carrot, American Ginseng, Wild Sarsaparilla, Prickly Ash, Mustard.

Stimulates appetite Yarrow, Polypody, Angelica, American Ginseng, Horseradish, Colicroot, Fennel, Caraway.

Stops bleeding, including menstrual and other internal bleeding, and from cuts and wounds. Plantain, Shepherd's Purse, Knotweed, Yarrow, Lady's Mantle, Horseweed, Purple Loosestrife, Silverweed, Cranesbill, Horsetail, Birthroot, Stinging Nettle, Witch Hazel.

Tonic Strengthens and restores the whole body. Silverweed, Eyebright, Horehound, Ground Ivy, Water Avens, American Ginseng, Sweet Flag, Stinging Nettle, Strawberry, Barberry, Dandelion, Blackberry.

Vitamin and mineral-rich plants Watercress, Blackcurrant, Roses, Barberry, Stinging Nettle, Carrot, Sheep Sorrel, Strawberry.

Plants which are useful for treating coughs, colds and flu include Garlic, Yarrow, Violet, Catnip, Polypody, Horehound, Ground Ivy, Boneset, Angelica, Wild Sarsaparilla, New Jersey Tea, Stinging Nettle, Watercress, Balm, Peppermint, St John's Wort, Woolly Mullein, Fennel, Coriander, Black Cherry, Willow, Sweet Gum, Elder, Sumac.

Plants which are useful for treating diarrhea include Purple Loosestrife, Silverweed, Sweet Goldenrod, Water Avens, Carrot, Wax Myrtle, Strawberry, Coriander, Woolly Mullein, Apple, Oak, Black Cherry, Slippery Elm, Blackberry, Raspberry.

Plants which are useful for promoting liver functions include Butter and Eggs, Agrimony, Chicory, Barberry, Cascara Sagrada, Dandelion.

Plants which are useful for alleviating rheumatism and arthritis include Yellow Sweet Clover, Horsemint, Sweet Goldenrod, Horseweed, Horsetail, Holly, Wild Yam, Flax, Wintergreen, Blackcurrant, Willow, Birch.

Plants which aid healing of cuts, sores and ulcers include Butter and Eggs, Yellow Sweet Clover, Silverweed, Cleavers, Agrimony, Lady's Mantle, Wild Sarsaparilla, Cranesbill, Horsetail, Birthroot, Strawberry, Pipsissewa, St John's Wort, Dogwood, Prickly Ash, Sweet Gum, Basswood, Birch, Raspberry.

Plants which make useful spring tonics include Watercress, Roses, Birch, Stinging Nettle, Sheep Sorrel.

Botanical Glossary

Annual A plant which grows from a seed, flowers, sets seed and dies in one year.
Axil The more-or-less V-shaped angle made by the junction between a leaf and a stem or twig.
Biennial A plant which forms leaves in the first year, produces a flowering shoot in the second year, flowers, sets seed and dies.
Bract A green leaf-like structure which has a flower in its axil, and which may remain on the plant with the fruit. Bracts vary enormously in size, shape and function.

Flower Structure

Flower Types

Flower Arrangement

Leaf Types

Simple leaves (not divided into leaflets)

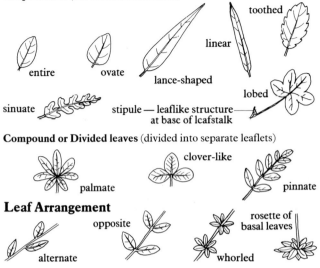

entire

ovate

lance-shaped

linear

toothed

lobed

sinuate

stipule — leaflike structure at base of leafstalk

Compound or Divided leaves (divided into separate leaflets)

palmate

clover-like

pinnate

Leaf Arrangement

alternate

opposite

whorled

rosette of basal leaves

Catkin A drooping spike of small flowers characteristic of some deciduous trees. Male catkins produce pollen; female catkins are pollinated and then develop into fruiting catkins which bear seeds.

Fruits contain the seeds. Different kinds of fruits include: **Berry** — a juicy fruit which usually contains several seeds; **Capsule** — a dry or fleshy fruit which splits open to release the seeds; **Nutlet** — a hard dry fruit containing a single seed; **Pod** — a long dry fruit, usually containing several large seeds, which splits open along one or both seams to release the seeds.

Node A point on a stem at which leaves are produced.

Perennial A plant which lives from year to year, starting into growth again each spring. Some perennial plants are herbaceous and die down each year, remaining dormant beneath the ground throughout the winter. Others are trees or shrubs; some lose their leaves in winter (**deciduous trees**), while others retain their leaves throughout the year and their growth slows down in winter (**evergreen trees**).

Rhizome A perennial underground stem which may look like a root.

Shoot A new young growth.

Tuber A swollen root or underground stem, which forms a food store for the plant.

A perennial plant with creeping underground stems and many erect, hairless flowering stems, clothed with linear, bright green leaves and with long terminal flower spikes. The flowers are like snapdragons, with orange palates and long straight spurs. Fruits are capsules containing winged, flattened seeds.

Found in disturbed and waste places, on roadsides and in fields, throughout the USA and much of Canada. Native to Europe.

Diuretic, purgative, astringent. An infusion can be used to treat jaundice, liver and gallbladder problems. It is also used as a diuretic to reduce water retention. Externally it can be used to bathe piles, also in an ointment to aid healing of sores and ulcers.

Parts used: whole plant, fresh or dried.

YELLOW SWEET CLOVER

A branched, more or less erect biennial plant. Its compound leaves each have three leaflets and a stipule at the base of the leaf stalk. The many flowers resemble yellow pea flowers and smell of new-mown hay; they grow in loose spikes on long stalks in the leaf axils. Pods are egg-shaped and brown.

Found on roadsides, in fields and waste places. Throughout the USA and much of Canada but commoner in the east and midwest than in the Pacific states; becoming rarer southward.

Emollient, carminative, antispasmodic, expectorant. An infusion can be used to relieve wind and to aid digestion. Externally it can be added to baths or used in compresses to treat boils, slow-healing cuts and bruises, or to relieve the pain of rheumatism and arthritis. Also used in eyewashes.

Parts used: leaves and flowers, dried in shade. Large doses can cause vomiting. White Sweet Clover can be used in the same way.

A perennial plant with long stems rooting at the nodes and forming rosettes of dark green, pinnate leaves with silver silky undersides. In the leaves, large leaflets alternate with small leaflets. Solitary, yellow, five-petalled flowers are borne on long stalks growing from the leaf axils.

Found in wet damp places, wet meadows and banks, on shores and beaches. Found across Canada to the arctic circle, south in northern areas of the USA and in the Rockies to New Mexico.

Astringent, tonic, antispasmodic. An infusion can be used as a remedy for diarrhea and abdominal cramps, also for alleviating painful periods. When added to bathwater, it will stop bleeding from piles and wounds. It can also be used as a gargle for sore throats and mouth ulcers.

Parts used: entire plant except the roots, dried in shade. The related plant, **Creeping Cinquefoil (1)** growing in the east in lawns and waste places, has also been used in herb medicine.

4–8in

A perennial, somewhat hairy plant with a clump of brittle stems and caustic orange sap. It has divided leaves with five to seven oval, toothed leaflets and loose clusters of yellow, four-petalled flowers in the upper leaf axils. Fruits are elongated capsules, each with a row of fleshy black seeds.

Found in moist soil, along roadsides and woodland edges, around buildings, from Quebec to Georgia, west to Iowa. Introduced from Europe and naturalized.

Diuretic, antispasmodic, sedative, purgative. An infusion can be taken to treat stomach spasms, indigestion, to promote the flow of bile and in the treatment of jaundice. Also used to relieve asthma. In ointments it can be used in the treatment of warts and ringworm.

Parts used: whole plant is used and should be dried quickly in shade. Strong doses are harmful, due to the caustic properties of the plant.

A perennial rosette-forming plant with many broad, rounded, almost hairless, long-stalked leaves, each up to 8in. long. The leaves have well-defined veins. Greenish flowers grow in spikes and have conspicuous anthers which are mauve at first, then yellowish. Fruiting spike has many small, hard fruits.

A very common weed throughout the USA and Canada, especially on bare trodden ground in waste places, back yards, on roadsides and tracks. Native of Europe.

Demulcent, expectorant, diuretic, astringent. The fresh leaves bring relief to minor cuts and stings, and stop bleeding. An infusion or fresh juice can be used to treat coughs and hoarseness, and to relieve gastritis.

Parts used: whole plant, fresh or dried. The related **English Plantain (1,)** with similar uses, has narrow upright leaves, long flower stems with short flower spikes and white anthers.

SHEPHERD'S PURSE

A small annual weed, with a rosette of tapering basal leaves, often deeply toothed and somewhat hairy. The leaves on the flower stalks have clasping bases. The tiny white flowers grow in small erect spikes. Each has four white, spoon-shaped petals. Fruits are heart-shaped pods, borne on long stalks.

A small but distinctive weed found in waste ground, back yards, roadsides and fields throughout the USA and much of Canada. Introduced from Europe.

Diuretic, stops bleeding. Fresh juice or an infusion of this herb can be used as a remedy, taken internally, for heavy menstrual bleeding and nosebleeds. It can also be used as a compress for cuts and wounds.

Parts used: whole plant can be used fresh or dried, except the roots. For drying, best collected in summer when partly in fruit and dried quickly; does not keep for more than a year.

CLEAVERS

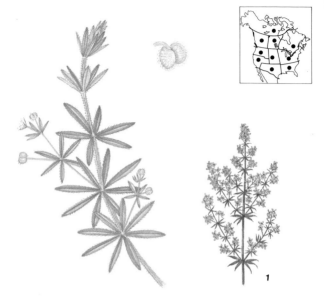

1

A scrambling annual plant with lax stems supported by other vegetation. Its four-angled stems have hooked bristles on the angles and linear bristly leaves, in whorls of six or eight. Clusters of tiny, tubular, whitish flowers grow in upper leaf axils, followed by pairs of small, rounded, hooked fruits.

Found in thickets, moist shady woodland and waste places throughout the USA and Canada, except the extreme north.

Diuretic, antispasmodic. An infusion can be used to stimulate the kidneys, to help the body eliminate excess water and to dispel kidney stones. It can also be used as a wash for bathing slow healing sores and cuts, and for treating skin infections.

Parts used: whole dried plant. **Lady's Bedstraw (1)** is another naturalized European plant which can be used in the same way.

A straggling, prostrate or erect annual plant with branched stems and alternate, lance-shaped leaves; leaves on main stems are larger than those on side stems. At the base of each leaf is a jagged, silvery sheath. Small pink flowers in leaf axils are followed by brown, three-sided fruits in dried petals.

A weed of waste places and cultivated ground, roadsides and yards, also found on shores and around salt marshes. Throughout North America.

Astringent, diuretic, stops bleeding. An infusion can be used for treating enteritis and diarrhea, also as a remedy for bleeding from ulcers and piles. The fresh juices can be used to stop bleeding from wounds and from nosebleeds. Knotweed tea, drunk regularly, helps to dispel kidney stones and gravel.

Parts used: fresh or dried flowering plant. **Smartweed (1)** is a related, larger plant; an infusion can be used to treat piles, ulcers and sores, and to dispel menstrual pain.

23

AGRIMONY

1–3ft

A perennial plant with an erect stem bearing pinnate leaves; and a terminal leafless flower spike, with many yellow, five-petalled flowers. The leaves have alternating pairs of large and small, toothed leaflets. Fruits are upside-down cones, covered with hooked bristles on the top.

Found in woods and fields, along roadsides in eastern USA, on the northern prairies and in Canada.

Astringent, antispasmodic, anti-inflammatory, diuretic, stops bleeding, promotes bile flow. An infusion can be used to treat gallstones and for other liver, spleen and kidney problems; also as a gargle and to treat diarrhea. A poultice made from fresh leaves and roots can be used to treat wounds and sores.

Parts used: dried whole plant before flowering, without the roots.

1–3ft

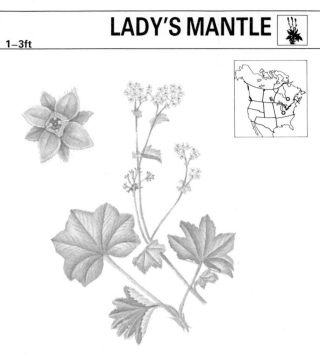

A perennial plant with a clump of large, long-stalked, palmately lobed leaves, more or less hairy. The tiny greenish yellow, petal-less flowers grow in terminal clusters on long, upright or sprawling flower stalks. A very variable plant.

Found in woodland and damp places, in southeastern Canada, New England and New York. Native in Labrador, introduced in the rest of its range.

Astringent, tonic, anti-inflammatory, antispasmodic, stops bleeding. An infusion can be drunk to prevent excessive menstrual bleeding, internal bleeding and diarrhea. Used externally as a poultice or for bathing, it stops bleeding and aids healing of infected wounds and sores.

Parts used: dried whole plant, collected when in flower, except the roots; the fresh roots can be used instead.

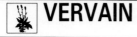

1

A perennial plant. The stiff, erect, rough stems are branched like a candlestick; they bear opposite pairs of large, lobed, dull green leaves and terminal spikes of flowers which lengthen as the fruits ripen. Each small tubular, lilac flower is followed by four red-brown nutlets, enclosed in its calyx.

Found in waste places, on roadsides and in fields in southeastern USA from Texas and Florida, north to Minnesota and Maine. Also in a few places in California. Native of Europe.

Astringent, diuretic, antispasmodic. An infusion can be used for treating coughs and nervous exhaustion, calming menstrual cramps and promoting milk production in nursing mothers. As a compress, it is used to treat headaches, neuralgia and rheumatism.

Parts used: whole dried plant. **Blue Vervain (1)** grows in much of North America. An infusion of leaves has been used to treat colds and chest infections, and to expel worms.

2–12in

A partially parasitic, annual plant. It forms a small clump of more or less erect, fine branched stems with toothed leaves. Two-lipped flowers are white, marked with purple and with yellow-spotted lower lips; each grows in the axil of a bract in a terminal spike. Fruits are capsules, cupped in sepals.

Found in fields, on roadsides and in waste places, from Newfoundland and Quebec south to Massachusetts and New York. Native of Europe.

Astringent, tonic. An infusion of the whole plant is a time-honored remedy for bathing tired eyes, and for treating styes, conjunctivitis and other eye inflammations. It can also be taken to alleviate the symptoms of colds and coughs.

Parts used: whole dried plant. Herbalists often combine Eyebright and **Goldenseal** in eye lotions.

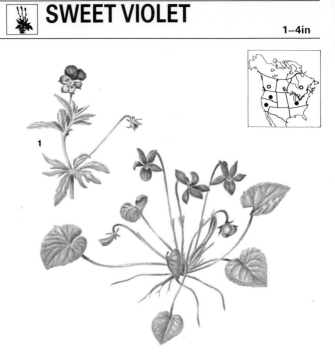

A small perennial plant, with long prostrate stems, rooting at the ends, and rosettes of long-stalked, broadly heart-shaped leaves. The sweet-scented flowers grow on long stalks; they are blue-violet or white, with long, pale violet spurs at the back. Fruits are rounded, hairy, three-part capsules.

Grown in gardens in northeastern and Pacific areas of the USA and across the border into Canada. It may escape and grow wild near dwellings in these areas. Native to Europe.

Expectorant, laxative. An infusion of leaves and flowers can be used as a mouthwash and gargle to soothe sore throats. With rootstock added, it can be used to treat bronchitis, coughs and whooping cough. The plant also has a soothing and calming effect. Roots are laxative; but large doses cause vomiting.

Parts used: dried leaves and flowers; fresh rootstock. Other violets are also useful medicinal herbs e.g. **Garden Pansy (1)** can be used to treat skin disorders and rheumatism.

A perennial plant with long creeping stems rooting at the nodes and opposite, hairy, kidney-shaped leaves which may turn red at the edges. The stems turn up at the ends to form inflorescences with whorls of flowers in upper leaf axils. The flowers are tubular and two-lipped, violet with purple spots.

Naturalized and found in shady places, on waste ground, on roadsides and in thickets in much of the USA and southern Canada. Absent or rarer in the south.

Diuretic, astringent, tonic. Contains Vitamin C. An infusion is helpful in relieving congestion in colds and bronchitis, especially when a kidney tonic is also needed. It can be used as a gargle for sore throats or as a wash for bathing cuts. It is particularly suitable for children.

Parts used: whole plant, fresh or dried. Young shoots can be used in soups or eaten like spinach.

HORSEMINT

1–3ft

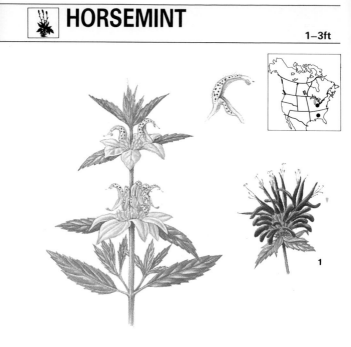

A perennial plant with erect four-angled stems and opposite lance-shaped leaves. The two-lipped, pale yellow, purple-spotted flowers grow in whorls in the axils of the upper leaves, with distinctive large, white-lilac, lance-shaped bracts around them.

Found in dry places and on sandy soils, on the coastal plain from New Jersey to Florida and Texas, also further west from Michigan and Minnesota south to Missouri.

Stimulant, carminative, diuretic, promotes sweating. Horsemint can be taken to relieve stomach problems like nausea and sickness, colic and flatulence; it can also be used to promote urine production. Oil of Horsemint, diluted with soap, can be rubbed on to alleviate the pains of rheumatism and backache.

Parts used: dried leaves and flowering tops. **Oswego Tea (1)** or Bergamot is a related plant, used to flavor commercial teas and in perfumery.

A grayish, scented perennial plant which forms a clump of branched leafy stems. It has oval to heart-shaped, wrinkled, toothed leaves, which are woolly white beneath. Dense spikes of purple-spotted white, two-lipped flowers grow on stalks in leaf axils.

Found in disturbed habitats throughout much of North America. Native to Europe.

Antispasmodic, carminative, tonic, promotes sweating. An infusion can be used to treat colds and chills and to bring a restful sleep. It can also be used as a remedy for colic, stomach acidity and flatulence, especially for children. It has also been used to stimulate menstruation.

Parts used: whole plant, fresh or dried.

MARJORAM

1–3ft

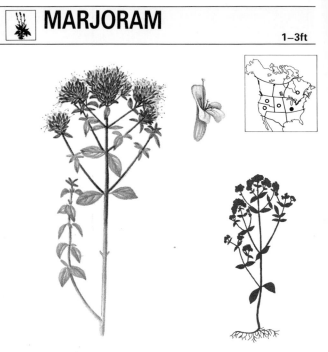

A hairy, aromatic perennial plant, with many erect four-angled stems and opposite oval leaves. Terminating the stems and borne on long stalks in the axils of the upper leaves are dense clusters of tiny rose-purple, two-lipped flowers. The flower clusters are partly hidden by purplish bracts.

Native to Europe, naturalized in disturbed areas, usually on calcareous soils, from Nova Scotia to Ontario, south to North Carolina and west to Oregon and California. Widely cultivated.

Sedative, antispasmodic, carminative, expectorant. Marjoram tea is a calming drink which can be taken to prevent insomnia, to soothe intestinal and menstrual cramps, to alleviate nervous upset stomach, headaches and coughs. It has been used to reduce seasickness. Marjoram oil relieves toothache.

Parts used: whole plant, fresh or dried. It is also used in perfumery. Sweet Marjoram (the kitchen herb) has similar properties.

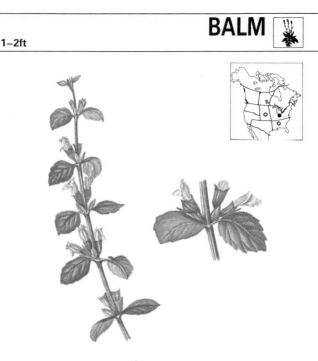

1–2ft

A lemon-scented, more or less hairy, perennial plant with spreading mats of leaves and erect branched flowering stems in summer. The stems bear opposite oval leaves with toothed margins, and whorls of white or pinkish, two-lipped flowers grow in the axils of the upper leaves.

Cultivated and found growing wild in fields and along roadsides in eastern USA, from Maine to Florida and west to Kansas.

Antispasmodic, carminative, promotes sweating, reduces fever. An infusion of balm makes a soothing drink that can be used to reduce anxiety, to calm nervous indigestion, to alleviate headaches, insomnia and menstrual cramps. It is also a cooling drink for feverish colds and flu, relieving catarrh.

Parts used: whole plant, fresh or dried, just before flowering. Balm is also used in pot-pourris and in the perfume industry.

1–2ft

A strongly scented perennial plant with a dense covering of white hairs. It has branched stems and opposite, rounded leaves with rounded teeth on the margins. Dense globular whorls of two-lipped, whitish flowers grow in toothed calyces in the axils of the upper leaves.

Found on roadsides, in disturbed and waste places in many parts of the USA and southern Canada. Native of Europe.

Expectorant, tonic, promotes bile flow. Most often given to children in the form of an infusion or a syrup for coughs and colds; it is also used as a remedy for bronchitis and hoarseness. Horehound tea can be used to alleviate the symptoms of the common cold and to stimulate the appetite.

Parts used: whole plant in flower, fresh or dried in shade.

MOTHERWORT

A softly hairy perennial plant with erect branched stems and opposite, palmately lobed leaves. Lower leaves have five to seven lobes, wedge-shaped upper ones have three lobes. Two-lipped, pink or white, purple-spotted, hairy flowers grow in whorls in upper leaf axils, making a long leafy flower spike.

Naturalized and found growing as a weed in much of the USA and southern Canada. Native to Europe.

Antispasmodic, sedative, promotes menstruation. The infusion is a useful tonic and sedative, especially for people with nervous heart problems, neuralgia and anxiety. It is also used to dispel wind and to soothe stomach cramps. It has been recommended for menopausal problems.

Parts used: whole flowering plant, dried in shade. Some people may have a skin reaction to touching the plant.

A creeping, scented perennial plant with woolly erect stems and soft, feathery leaves. The white or pink-tinged flowers are borne in large, flat, dense clusters, on top of the erect stems. Each flower head resembles a single flower but has five ray florets and a central disk. Seeds have small wings.

Found in fields and grassy places, in waste ground and on roadsides throughout North America, except the far north. Both native and introduced European forms are present.

Astringent, antispasmodic, tonic, promotes sweating. Yarrow tea is a remedy for colds. It is also used to stimulate the appetite, to treat liver disorders and to cut down menstrual bleeding. As a wash, it can be used to stop bleeding from piles, nosebleeds and cuts, and to soothe sores and bruises.

Parts used: whole plant in flower, dried in shade. Camomile, a European plant grown in gardens, is used to make a soothing and sedative tea, which may be used to alleviate insomnia.

SWEET GOLDENROD

A perennial plant, with an erect stem. Alternate leaves grow on lower part of the stem; they are smooth, stalkless, long and narrow with many translucent dots and a scent of aniseed when crushed. The yellow flower heads are crowded on arching branches on the upper part of the stem.

Found in dry open woods and fields, often in sandy soils, from New England to Florida, west to Missouri and Texas.

Astringent, carminative, stimulant, diuretic, promotes sweating. An infusion of the leaves and flowers can be used to alleviate flatulence and to promote sweating in fevers. An infusion of flowers has been used to treat kidney gravel and dropsy.

Parts used: dried leaves and flowers. The dried leaves are also used to make tea. The leaves of Canadian Goldenrod can be used as dressings for wounds and bruises.

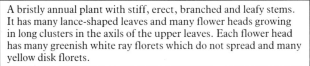

A bristly annual plant with stiff, erect, branched and leafy stems. It has many lance-shaped leaves and many flower heads growing in long clusters in the axils of the upper leaves. Each flower head has many greenish white ray florets which do not spread and many yellow disk florets.

A common weed of waste places, roadsides and fields found throughout the USA and southern Canada.

Astringent, diuretic, tonic. An infusion of the whole dried plant can be used to treat diarrhea, dysentery and internal or menstrual bleeding. It is also used as a remedy for piles and its diuretic properties make it useful in the treatment of rheumatism, kidney gravel and dropsy.

Parts used: whole plant in flower, dried in bunches.

1

A perennial plant with an erect, stout, hairy stem branched at the top and opposite, lance-shaped leaves, joined across the stem at their bases. The leaves are 4–8in. long. The fuzzy white flower heads are borne in dense, flat-topped clusters terminating the stems.

Found in moist meadows, low-lying damp ground and wet woods from Nova Scotia and Quebec to Florida, and west to Minnesota and Louisiana.

Stimulant, laxative, promotes sweating, reduces fever. A warm infusion can be used to treat colds and flu, especially to reduce the fever. Taken cold, it acts as a tonic and mild laxative. In hot strong doses, it causes vomiting and acts as a purgative.

Parts used: dried leaves and flowering tops. An infusion of the roots of the related **Joe-Pye Weed** (1) can be used as a diuretic, to treat kidney gravel, gout and rheumatism.

An erect, hairy perennial plant, with a clump of unbranched, four-angled, tall leafy stems. The lance-shaped leaves grow in opposite pairs or in whorls of three, their bases clasping the stems. Whorls of purple, six-petalled flowers grow in the axils of the upper leaves, forming a tall flower spike.

Found along the shores of lakes and rivers, in wet meadows, marshes and roadside ditches. From Newfoundland to Minnesota and south to Virginia and Missouri. Introduced from Europe.

Astringent, stops bleeding. An infusion can be used to stop dysentery and diarrhea, even in serious illnesses like typhoid or in babies, also as a remedy for enteritis and internal bleeding. A cold compress of the herb stops bleeding from wounds and cuts, helps bruises and sores to heal.

Parts used: the whole plant, fresh or dried in shade.

COMMON HORSETAIL

8in–3ft

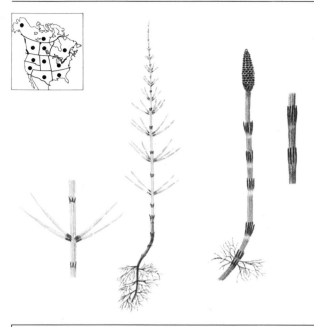

A perennial plant with creeping underground stems. From these in summer grow jointed, grooved, sterile stems with whorls of jointed branches. At each joint there is a toothed sheath with black tips on the teeth. Brown jointed fertile stems appear before the sterile stems; they bear terminal cones.

Found in damp places, in fields and meadows, woods, on roadsides; it can be a persistent weed. Throughout North America.

Diuretic, astringent, stops bleeding. An infusion can be used as a wash for stopping bleeding from cuts, to aid healing of sores and as a gargle. It can also be taken internally to treat kidney stones and stop internal bleeding, and to alleviate coughs, rheumatism and arthritis.

Parts used: sterile stems, best used fresh but can be dried. Several other horsetails, like the Wood Horsetail which grows in damp woods on acid soils, have been used in herb medicine.

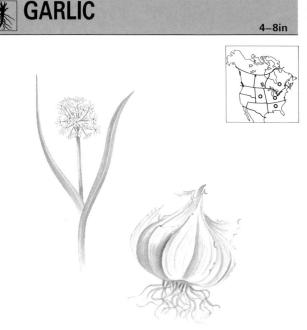

Underground bulbs are small, with many bulblets (or cloves) closely swathed in white scales. The leaves are flat and grass-like, strongly scented like the bulbs. The flowers grow with small bulbils in loose umbels on long leafless stalks. In bud, each umbel is enclosed in a pointed membrane.

Widely cultivated and grown in kitchen gardens throughout much of the USA and in southern Canada. Occasionally found growing wild.

Diuretic, antiseptic, stimulant, expectorant, promotes sweating. Raw garlic juice is an effective antiseptic for wounds. It is used to treat bronchitis, colds and flu, to promote digestion and relieve wind and stomach cramps, and to improve blood circulation. It also helps to expel worms.

Parts used: bulbs or the juice from the bulbs. Related wild North American species, like the Prairie Onion, were used by the Indians for food and in their herbal remedies.

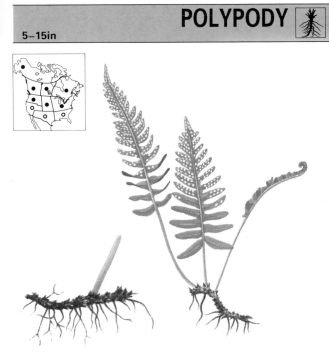

A small fern with a creeping, scaly red-brown rhizome. From this grow many single, long-stalked, deeply lobed leaves (or fronds;) the lobes are elongated and the furthest lobes are smallest. On the back of each lobe is a double row of round spore-bearing structures, ripening bright yellow.

Found in shady areas, on rocks and banks, sometimes on logs. Throughout much of North America, but much rarer in the south.

Expectorant, demulcent, purgative, kills worms. An infusion of chopped rhizome can be used to treat catarrh, coughs and other respiratory problems and to stimulate appetite. A stronger brew acts as a mild laxative and kills worms. As a wash, it can be used to bathe wounds.

Parts used; rhizome, cleaned and dried. Other ferns are used in herbal medicine, including Male Fern which is used to expel worms and Royal Fern which is used to treat liver disorders.

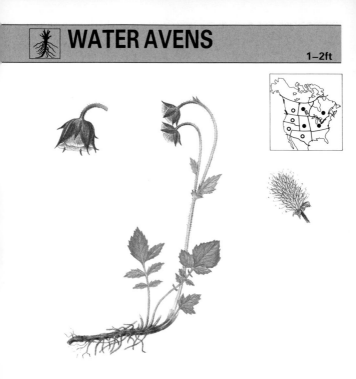

A perennial plant, with a rosette of long-stalked, pinnate leaves. Each leaf has a few pairs of small, toothed leaflets and a larger terminal three-lobed leaflet. Nodding flowers have purple sepals and yellowish, purple-veined petals; they grow on branched stalks and are followed by hooked fruits.

Found in wet meadows and swamps from Newfoundland to B.C., south to New Jersey in the east, to Missouri, and to New Mexico in the west.

Astringent, digestive, tonic. An infusion of the dried root can be used to treat diarrhea and dysentery. It is also used as a remedy for dyspepsia, to improve digestion and to stimulate appetite.

Parts used: dried rhizome. Also called Chocolate Root, it was once used as substitute for cocoa. White Avens, a white-flowered plant from eastern woods, has similar properties.

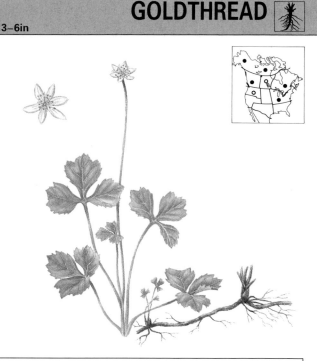

A small perennial plant with thin, bright yellow, creeping rhizomes. It forms clumps of long-stalked, shiny evergreen leaves, each with three toothed leaflets. The solitary white flowers grow on long stalks; each has five to seven petals and many stamens. Fruits are pod-like.

Found in cool damp woods and bogs across northern Canada, south in the east to Indiana.

Stimulates appetite, sedative. The liquid obtained from boiling the underground stems in water can be used as a gargle for a sore throat or ulcerated mouth, or as an eyewash for sore eyes. It has also been used to alleviate dyspepsia and is said to help people combat the craving for alcohol.

Parts used: dried rhizomes. These can be boiled or chewed to alleviate mouth sores. Also known an Canker-root, from its medicinal uses.

A perennial hairless plant, with very long, fleshy taproots, rosettes of large, long-stalked, ovate leaves and robust, erect leafy stems. It has many white four-petalled flowers in a much-branched leafy inflorescence, which elongates as it ages. The fruits are round pods on long, upright stalks.

Cultivated throughout much of North America; it grows as an escape around buildings and in yards, as it has very persistent roots.

Stimulant and stimulates appetite, rubefacient, diuretic. Can be used in poultices, like mustard, to ease congestion of bronchitis and chest infections, rheumatism etc., or as an infusion in treatment of kidney stones and dropsy. Fresh juice stimulates digestion and acts as a tonic to the whole system.

Parts used: fresh roots (they can be stored in the fridge,) but it must be used in small quantities only. Too strong a dose will cause vomiting.

A robust, scented perennial with smooth purple stems and large compound basal leaves. The leaves have leafstalks with sheathing bases and large toothed leaflets. White flowers grow in large, compound, rounded umbels, each with 20–45 stalks. Oval fruits are ridged with thin lateral wings.

Found in marshes and swamps, wet woods and river banks. From Labrador to Minnesota, south to Delaware and Iowa.

Stimulates appetite, carminative, expectorant, diuretic. An infusion of the dried root can be used as remedy for coughs and colds, to stimulate appetite, to dispel wind and to soothe intestinal cramps. Also used to stimulate the kidneys. The wash is used to relieve rheumatism and neuralgia.

Parts used: dried rhizome. Also called Chocolate Root, it was once used as substitute for cocoa. White Avens, white-flowered plant from eastern woods, has similar properties.

A biennial plant with a rosette of ferny leaves in the first year and a stout taproot. In the second year a leafy flowering stem bears tight terminal umbels of white flowers. There is often one reddish flower in the center of each umbel. In "fruit" the umbels become cup-like and contain spiky fruits.

Cultivated throughout much of the USA and southern Canada. Also grows as a weed in open dry places and roadsides, fields and waste places in this region. Native of Eurasia.

Diuretic, carminative, stimulant. Contains carotene, the precursor of Vitamin A and essential for good vision. Easily digested and an effective remedy for wind and other intestinal problems, diarrhea and roundworms. Stimulates the kidneys. A poultice of carrot pulp is good for burns, ulcers and eczema.

Parts used: usually the fresh root, but also powdered root. Cultivated carrots have fleshy roots; Wild Carrots may have tough roots and must not be mistaken for Poison Hemlock.

PARSLEY

1–2ft

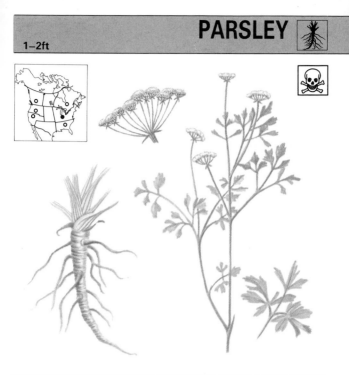

An erect, hairless perennial plant with a distinctive scent. It has shiny, pinnate leaves with triangular-lobed leaflets, often curled in cultivated plants. The small yellowish flowers grow in flat-topped, compound umbels, each with 8–15 smaller umbels. Fruits are egg-shaped, ridged, somewhat flattened.

Cultivated and occasionally found growing wild in waste places or around buildings in eastern and Pacific areas of the USA and Canada.

Antispasmodic, carminative, diuretic, expectorant, promotes menstruation. Parsley tea, made with seeds and leaves, or with the root, promotes kidney action and can be used to treat gravel and stones; also to treat dropsy and jaundice. It aids digestion and dispels wind. It also makes a good eyewash.

Parts used: roots, fresh or dried, and seeds; leaves contain Vitamin C. Best grown in the garden rather than gathered wild, since it resembles poisonous wild plants like Poison Hemlock.

A perennial, slow-growing plant with a large spindle-shaped, fleshy root and a smooth erect stem. At the top of the stem are three large palmate leaves, each with five long-stalked, pointed-oblong leaflets. In the leaf axil grows an umbel of yellow-green, scented flowers, followed by red berries.

Found in moist rich woods, originally from Quebec and Nova Scotia to Minnesota and Pennsylvania, south in the mountains to Georgia. Now an endangered species in much of this area.

Tonic, demulcent. A tea made from infusing the powdered root acts as a mild stimulant, stimulates the appetite and may help soothe nervous indigestion. It is also thought to help prevent coughs and colds. For centuries in China, this was considered an almost magical drug, a cure for many bodily woes.

Parts used: dried roots. Rare over much of its former range because it grows slowly and has been overcollected; wild plants should be left alone. Also cultivated in some areas.

A perennial plant with a long, creeping, fleshy rhizome from which grow large, long-stalked compound leaves. Each leaf has three sections, subdivided into three or five pointed-ovate leaflets. Umbels of greenish white flowers grow on separate shorter stalks, followed by purple-black berries.

Found in woodlands in southern Canada from Newfoundland to B.C. and south, east of the Rocky Mountains to Georgia and Colorado, in mountains in southern parts of its range.

Stimulant, promotes sweating. An infusion can be used to treat asthma and coughs, as well as being effective against rheumatism. As a wash it can be used to bathe ulcers, wounds and shingles, or the dried rhizome can be made into a poultice for external use.

Parts used: dried rhizome. Spikenard, a related plant with flowers and leaves borne on the same stalks, can be used in the same ways.

51

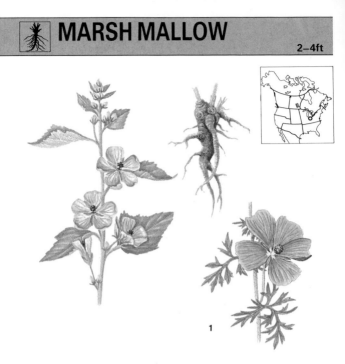

1

A densely velvety, gray-white perennial plant with erect leafy stems and a thick taproot. The lower leaves are long-stalked and lobed, upper ones folded like a fan. The pale pink flowers grow in small clusters in leaf axils of upper leaves; they have velvety sepals. Fruits are brown-green, downy nutlets.

Found in salt marshes on the Atlantic coast, less commonly inland on damp, saline soils, in wet places. Also cultivated. Quebec to Virginia. Native to Europe.

Emollient, demulcent, anti-inflammatory. The mucilage produced when the roots are boiled is used for soothing inflammation of the digestive system and kidneys. Also used as a gargle for sore throats and mouths, and in treating chest infections; and externally as a poultice for burns, cuts and boils.

Parts used: dried roots, also dried leaves and flowers. The leaves and flowers of **Musk Mallow** (1) and High Mallow have the same properties but are less effective.

SPOTTED CRANESBILL

1–2ft

A perennial plant with a thick rhizome and long-stalked, palmately divided basal leaves. Bowl-shaped flowers are rose-purple with five petals; they grow in small terminal clusters, on long stalks in the axils of stem leaves. Fruits are like five-part beaks, which split into spoon-shaped sections.

Found in woods and thickets, on shady roadsides and in meadows from Manitoba to southern Ontario, south to Georgia and Arkansas; west to Kansas.

Astringent, stops bleeding. An infusion can be used to treat diarrhea and internal bleeding, or used as a mouthwash to alleviate sore throats, sore gums, ulcers and bleeding in the mouth, or used as an eyewash. It is also an effective treatment for piles and is used to stop bleeding from cuts.

Parts used: dried rhizome. The dried leaves of the related Herb Robert, a European plant widely naturalized in the east, can be used for the same purposes.

53

VALERIAN

A perennial almost hairless plant with a clump of erect leafy stems. Leaves are opposite, pinnate with lance-shaped, toothed leaflets. Pale pink, tubular flowers grow in three-forked terminal heads. Each flower has a small, inrolled calyx at the base; as the fruits form, calyces become feathery parachutes.

Grown in gardens (where they are called Garden Heliotropes) and naturalized in fields and roadsides from Quebec to Minnesota and south to New Jersey and Ohio. Native to Europe.

Antispasmodic, soothes nerves. An infusion made from the roots soothes nervous fatigue, headaches and neuralgia, and relieves insomnia. It can be used for alleviating the symptoms of stress. Valerian should not be used for more than two or three weeks at a time, as it may then be harmful or become addictive.

Parts used: dried roots. Valerian roots are grown commercially and used in proprietary medicines in Europe. Other valerians are not generally used in herb medicine.

CONEFLOWER

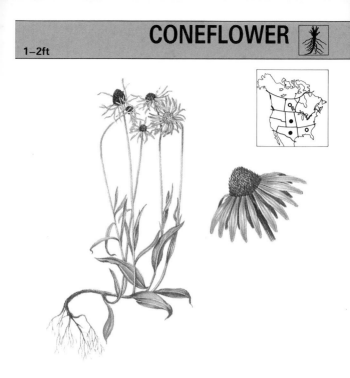

A perennial plant with a woody rhizome and an erect bristly stem. The stem bears alternate, lance-shaped bristly leaves, the lower leaves with long stalks. The single flower has drooping or spreading purple ray florets and yellow disk florets.

Found in dry open ground and on the prairies from Saskatchewan and Manitoba to Colorado, Texas and Tennessee in the east.

Antiseptic, improves general health by increasing resistance to infection. The liquid obtained from boiling the dried rhizome in water can be drunk to purify the blood and is thus a good remedy for boils, abscesses and other infections, acne and eczema.

Parts used: dried rhizome. The related Purple Coneflower has similar medicinal properties.

A small rosette-forming perennial plant with a long thin taproot and a clump of entire or sinuate leaves. All parts are filled with white milky juice. Bright yellow flower heads grow singly on long, hollow, leafless stalks. Seeds form "clocks," round balls of seeds with parachutes of hairs.

A familiar weed of lawns and back yards, roadsides and other grassy places, in waste ground. Throughout the USA and southern Canada. Native of Europe.

Diuretic, tonic. An infusion of roots can be used to promote the flow of bile and stimulate liver function. Also used to stimulate kidney function and to help eliminate excess water. It is also used as a gentle remedy for stomach disorders and dyspepsia, and to promote digestion.

Parts used: roots and young leaves. Fresh dandelion juice makes a good spring tonic. The leaves can be used in salads and the flowers to make wine.

A perennial plant with a large taproot and a clump of tough, branched stems, often roughly hairy. The leaves are deeply lobed with wavy, toothed edges, upper ones simpler than lower ones. Bright blue flower heads grow in small clusters in upper leaf axils; they open in the morning. Seeds are pale brown.

Found on roadsides, in vacant lots, waste ground and fields throughout the USA and Canada. Native to Europe.

Digestive, promotes production of bile. The liquid obtained from boiling the chopped roots can be used as a remedy for sluggish liver functioning and for gallstones. It is also used for treating dyspepsia.

Parts used: roots, chopped and dried. Roasted chicory roots may be used as a substitute for coffee and the young leaves eaten in salads.

57

A perennial plant with a short thick rhizome and erect stems. Each stem bears a terminal whorl of three broad diamond-shaped leaves and one unpleasantly scented, purplish brown, terminal flower. The flower grows on a short stalk in the center of the whorl of leaves; it has three petals and three sepals.

Found in moist woodland from Nova Scotia and Quebec to Ontario and Michigan, south to Georgia; in the mountains in the southern part of its range.

Astringent, antiseptic, expectorant. The liquid obtained from boiling the dried rhizome in water can be used to bathe wounds and stop bleeding, and to treat skin irritations and ulcers. In the past this remedy was used to stop bleeding after childbirth and to treat menstrual problems.

Parts used: dried rhizome. Also known as Purple Trillium or Wake Robin; other Trilliums, like red-flowered Toadshade and white Large-flowered Trillium also have medicinal properties.

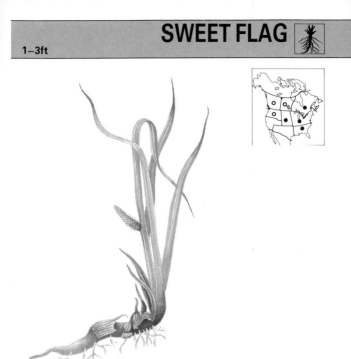

A perennial plant with a swollen creeping rhizome and flat sword-like leaves. The leaves have distinctive wavy margins, thick midribs and smell of tangerines when bruised. Green flowers grow in crowded spikes, the spike growing at an angle of 45° about a third of the way up a flattened leaf-like stalk.

Found in shallow water in swamps and on the margins of streams and rivers, where the rhizomes grow in mud. Across southern Canada, south to Florida and Colorado.

Carminative, digestive, tonic. An infusion of the chopped rhizome is an old remedy for dyspepsia, flatulence and acid indigestion, or the root may simply be chewed to alleviate such symptoms. It is also used to stimulate the appetite.

Parts used: dried rhizome. The rhizome may be candied or used as a spice. Calamus oil, extracted from the rhizome, is used in perfumery and in the making of some beers.

⚘ COLICROOT

1–3ft

A perennial plant with a basal clump of long lance-shaped, pointed leaves and an erect flowering stalk. The flowers grow in a long spike terminating the flower stalk; each is white and urn-shaped. They are followed by capsules enclosed in the withered flowers.

Found in open woods and barrens, in acid sandy or peaty soils. From Maine to Minnesota and Ontario, south to Florida and Texas.

Stimulates appetite. The liquid obtained from boiling the dried roots can be used as a treatment for wind, dyspepsia and colic. It has also been used as a general tonic and to prevent cramps in menstruation.

Parts used: dried roots. Fresh roots should not be used since they contain substances which cause dizziness, intestinal cramps and sickness. These substances are lost in drying.

WILD YAM

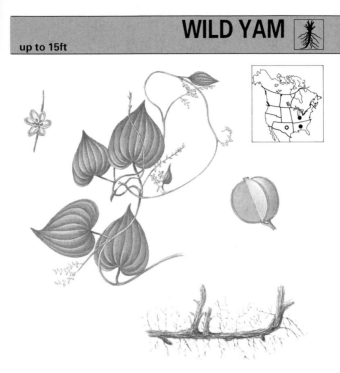

A perennial vine with long, knotted, contorted, woody roots and twining stems. The heart-shaped leaves grow alternately on long stalks. Clusters of tiny green-white flowers grow on branched stalks from the axils of the leaves, male and female on separate plants. Fruits are triangular winged capsules.

Grows twining over fences and hedges, over trees and shrubs in woods and thickets, from New York to Minnesota and south to Florida and Texas.

Antispasmodic, diuretic, expectorant. An infusion of the dried root can be used to alleviate bilious colic, especially in pregnancy. It contains steroid-like substances and this may explain why it relieves rheumatism and other inflammations. It can also be taken to relieve muscle spasms and neuralgia.

Parts used: dried roots.

61

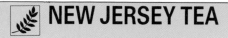

A low bushy shrub with thin, densely hairy, red-brown twigs and alternately arranged, deciduous leaves. The leaves are simple with fine teeth on the edges and three prominent ribs. Tiny white flowers grow in dense, cylindrical clusters in the leaf axils. The roots are large and red-brown in color.

Found in open woods at low elevations, in well-drained coarse soils in eastern USA, west to Kansas and into the prairies, and north into eastern Canada.

Astringent, antispasmodic, expectorant, sedative. An infusion of dried root bark can be taken to alleviate asthma, chronic bronchitis and whooping cough. It can be used as a gargle for sore throat and tonsillitis.

Parts used: dried bark from the roots. The dried leaves from this plant are used to make tea. The leaves of the related Mountain Balm, from the Rockies, are also used to make tea.

up to 30ft

An evergreen shrub or small tree with smooth, light gray bark. Its leaves are lance-shaped with a few teeth, shiny yellow-green and stiff, fragrant when rubbed. Male and female catkins appear on separate plants in spring. The fruits which follow are clusters of warty berries, covered in blue-white wax.

Found in moist sandy soil, in swamps and brackish marshes, in pine barrens and along ponds and lakes. In the coastal plain from New Jersey to Texas and north to Arkansas.

Stimulant, astringent; emetic in large doses. The liquid obtained from boiling the root bark can be used to treat diarrhea and dysentery, also as a gargle for inflamed gums and tonsils and sore throat. A poultice made from the root bark can be used to aid healing of wounds and bruises.

Parts used: dried bark of roots. The wax from the berries also has astringent properties.

SCOTCH PINE

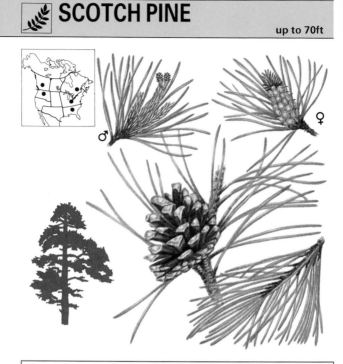

A tall pine tree, with broad stiff, usually twisted, blue-green needles, 1–3in. long, growing in pairs. The bark of the upper trunk and branches is bright orange-brown, bark of lower trunk dark brown and fissured. The cones are pointed egg-shaped, dull gray-brown in color, 2–3in. long.

Planted in cities, shelterbelts and plantations in the east and on the west coast. This tree is native to northern Europe but is now grown in many of the temperate areas of the world.

Rubefacient, diuretic, expectorant, irritant, antiseptic. It can be used as an inhalant or infusion to treat chest infections, catarrh and asthma. Can also be added to the bath for the treatment of fatigue, sleeplessness, skin disorders and irritations, small wounds and cuts.

Parts used: young shoots and buds, when sticky with resin, especially in spring. They should be kept in a dry place. The inner bark of native White Pine is used in cough medicines.

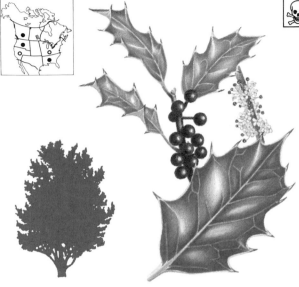

An evergreen shrub or small tree with smooth gray bark. The leaves are alternate and are quite characteristic, dark glossy green above and paler beneath, with spiny-sinuous edges. White fragrant flowers grow in small clusters in the leaf axils and are followed by clusters of round red berries in midwinter.

The familiar holly grown in North America from B.C. to California and from New Jersey to Oklahoma, most common on the north Pacific coast. Several native hollies grow in the east.

Astringent, expectorant, reduces fever. The liquid obtained from boiling holly leaves in water can be used to reduce fever and treat colds and flu. It can also be used as a remedy for bronchitis, arthritis and rheumatism.

Parts used: young leaves, fresh or dried. The berries are poisonous, inducing violent vomiting. The leaves of several native hollies also reduce fever and contain caffeine.

65

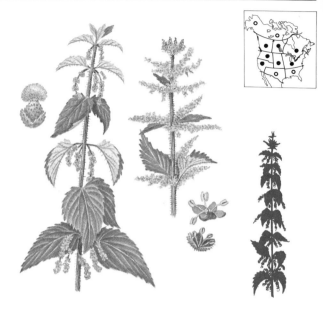

A large perennial plant, clothed in stinging hairs. It has a clump of upright, four-angled stems bearing pairs of roughly toothed, deep green pointed leaves. Small, petal-less flowers grow in "tassels" in leaf axils, male and female on separate plants. Fruits are small nutlets enclosed in dried sepals.

Found in woods, in waste places, on roadsides and on cultivated land in eastern and central USA and in most of Canada, except the far north. Native of Europe.

Diuretic, tonic, stimulates lactation. Contains magnesium, iron, Vitamin C. Fresh juice from young shoots is a good spring tonic. The liquid obtained from boiling them in water can be used to treat rheumatism, colds and bronchitis, to diminish menstrual and other bleeding and to stop diarrhea.

Parts used: young shoots and leaves, fresh or dried. The shoots can be used as a green vegetable; they must be gathered with care but cooking or infusing destroys the stinging hairs.

WATERCRESS

A succulent perennial plant with weak stems which root at the nodes and then turn upwards to form leafy shoots. Alternate leaves are compound, dark green. White or pale purple four-petalled flowers are borne in loose spikes. Fruits are slender pods with two rows of seeds, borne more or less upright.

Found in running water, streams and springs throughout the USA and some parts of southern Canada. Widely cultivated for use in salads. Introduced from Europe.

Diuretic, expectorant. With its high Vitamin C, iron and minerals content, the diluted juice of this plant is very useful as a spring tonic; it is also effective in the treatment of coughs, catarrh and bronchitis. It can be used to treat disorders of the kidney and bladder.

Parts used: fresh leaves and shoots, available throughout the year, and can be added to salads. Excessive or prolonged use may cause stomach upset and lead to kidney problems.

SHEEP SORREL

An annual or perennial plant, with a clump of dark green, arrow-shaped basal leaves and an erect, leafy flowering stem. Tiny green or reddish flowers grow in whorls in narrow elongated spikes and are followed by tiny, shiny brown, three-angled nutlets enclosed by calyces.

Found in disturbed ground, on roadsides and in yards, in grassland and fields, usually on acid soils. Throughout much of the USA and Canada, except the far north and south.

Astringent, diuretic, reduces fever. Contains Vitamin C. An infusion of fresh leaves is a cooling drink that allays thirst and reduces fever. It is a useful spring tonic. It is not recommended for anyone suffering from rheumatism, gout or kidney stones, as it contains oxalic acid.

Parts used: fresh young leaves and shoots. Can also be used in salads. The larger Garden Sorrel has the same uses and is stronger.

PEPPERMINT

1–3ft

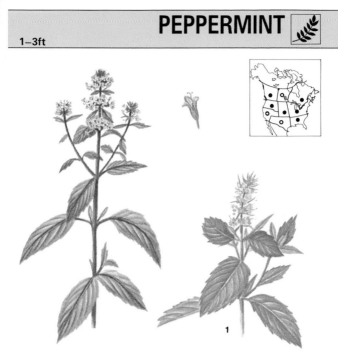

1

A perennial plant, smelling and tasting of peppermint. It forms erect, reddish, four-angled, branched stems with toothed, lance-shaped leaves. In the axils of the upper leaves are dense spikes of tiny reddish lilac, sterile flowers, arranged in whorls.

Cultivated throughout much of the USA and southern Canada. In many areas it has escaped from cultivation and become naturalized in wet places.

Antispasmodic, carminative, antiseptic, anaesthetic, relieves pain. Peppermint tea aids digestion, relieves wind and calms intestinal cramps, nausea and heartburn. It soothes coughs and colds, anxiety and insomnia. Used in salves, it is cooling and can be used to relieve the pain of headaches and rheumatism.

Parts used: fresh or dried leaves. Used commercially in many teas, medicines, salves, inhalants etc. **Spearmint (1,)** the garden mint made into mint jelly, has similar properties.

A biennial or perennial plant with many leafy branches and many flower heads. The leaves are alternate, oblong and toothed, the upper ones clasping the stems. Flower heads are about an inch across when open; they are sticky and yellow and the bracts which surround them are rolled back.

Found in open and dry areas, on roadsides and waste land and often a weed of rangeland. B.C. to Minnesota and south to California and Texas.

Expectorant, antispasmodic, sedative. An infusion can be used to alleviate coughs and bronchitis, asthma and whooping cough. It has also been used to treat catarrhal kidney problems and cystitis. Also used as a wash for burns, skin irritation or inflammation, or to treat the effects of poison ivy.

Parts used: dried leaves or flowering tops. This plant absorbs selenium from the soil and becomes toxic in areas where the soil is rich in selenium; do not pick it from such areas.

3–6ft

A perennial plant with an erect, slightly hairy stem and compound leaves. Each leaf has 4–8 pairs of elliptical leaflets. The flowers grow in clusters in the leaf axils; they are yellow with five somewhat unequal petals. The flowers are followed by long brown hairless pods with many seeds.

Found in open woods and beside streams from Pennsylvania across to Iowa and south to Florida and Texas.

Laxative, kills worms. An infusion of dried leaves (mixed with cloves or ginger and cream of tartar to prevent the griping it causes when given alone) is an effective laxative. No more than two cups in a day should be taken since this could cause nausea, griping pains and purging of the bowels.

Parts used: dried leaves. Commercial senna comes from a related Arabian plant.

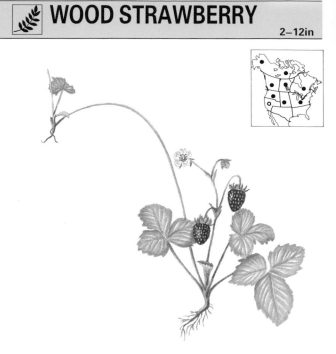

A small, perennial plant with long runners. These root at the nodes to form tufts of long-stalked, hairy leaves, each with three toothed leaflets. Small, flat clusters of white five-petalled flowers grow on long stalks. The sepals are joined together behind each flower. Fruits are small strawberries.

Found in woods and meadows across Canada, south to Virginia and Iowa and in the Rockies from Alaska to New Mexico.

Astringent, diuretic, tonic. Tea made with the leaves can be used to counter diarrhea, stomach upsets and disorders of the liver. Poultices of leaves can be used to treat ulcers and infected wounds. Fruits contain Vitamin C, and are effective in reducing fever. Fresh juice can be used to clean the skin.

Parts used: dried young leaves and roots; fruits. Garden strawberries are less effective.

A trailing or prostrate evergreen shrub, with mats of leafy stems. The simple leaves are smooth and leathery, wedge-shaped and tapering to the base. Terminal clusters of white, pink-tinged, urn-shaped flowers give rise to red, mealy, berry-like fruits.

Found in sandy or rocky areas with acid soil, in arctic areas from Labrador to Alaska and locally further south to northern areas of the USA.

Astringent, diuretic, tonic. An infusion of dried leaves can be used as an effective short-term remedy for kidney stones and gravel. Since it is antiseptic it is also used to treat cystitis. Long-term use can lead to stomach distress and poisoning and is not advisable.

Parts used: dried leaves. These are also used as a substitute for tobacco by Indians, who call the plant Kinnikinnick.

73

A small half-shrubby plant with creeping underground stems and erect stems with evergreen leaves. The leaves are thick and shiny, dark green and toothed, and grow in whorls on the erect stems. Nodding, waxy flowers grow in terminal clusters; each is white or pink, with five petals and a ring of red anthers.

Found in dry woods throughout much of the USA and southern Canada, in the mountains in the south. Absent from the southeastern and central southern states.

Astringent, diuretic, tonic. Tea made from infusing the leaves can be used in the treatment of rheumatism, kidney gravel and stones, and dropsy. It is also useful as a wash for skin diseases, ulcers and sores.

Parts used: leafy part of plant, fresh or dried. An infusion of the leaves of Spotted Wintergreen, a similar related plant with white-mottled leaves, can be used as a diuretic.

2–6in

A creeping evergreen shrub with erect stems and aromatic, shiny oval leaves near the tops of the stems. White, bell-shaped, nodding flowers grow in the axils of the leaves and are followed by bright red berries.

Forms spreading patches under large shrubs and trees, on sandy acid soils. From Newfoundland to Manitoba and Minnesota, south to Kentucky, in the mountains to Georgia.

Astringent, stimulant, carminative, diuretic, relieves pain. Tea made from Wintergreen leaves is a traditional pain reliever and is used to alleviate headaches, rheumatism and arthritis. Oil of wintergreen can be used externally to relieve muscular pain, sciatica, lumbago, pain in joints etc.

Parts used: leaves. Pure Oil of wintergreen can cause skin irritation and must be used with caution. It is poisonous except in very small amounts. It is used to flavor toothpaste.

A biennial plant with a rosette of large, woolly leaves in the first year and a tall flowering stem in the second. Stem leaves are woolly with many star-shaped hairs and their bases run down the stem. The flowering stem is crowded with yellow flowers, opening a few at a time. Fruits are woolly capsules.

Found on roadsides, in waste places and in fields throughout the USA and southern Canada. Native of Europe.

Demulcent, emollient, astringent, expectorant. An infusion of dried flowers is used to soothe asthma, coughs, bronchitis, whooping cough and tonsillitis. It is also used for treating intestinal cramps and diarrhea, and for bathing wounds and skin inflammations. Mullein oil is used for treating earache.

Parts used: dried flowers or leaves. Other mulleins can be used in the same way, like Moth Mullein and Orange Mullein, both naturalized European species.

COMMON ST JOHN'S WORT

1–3ft

A hairless, branched perennial plant, spreading by leafy offshoots.
The stems bear many opposite, stalkless ovate leaves, marked
with translucent dots, and many flowers in branched clusters.
Each flower has five yellow petals with black dots on the margins
and many yellow stamens.

Found on roadsides, fields and waste places and a weed in some
places. Throughout much of the USA and southern Canada.
Introduced from Europe.

Astringent, antispasmodic, expectorant, sedative and stimulates
digestion. In an infusion, its sedative effect can be used for
treating bedwetting and insomnia. It is also used to treat coughs
and chest infections, and gastric disorders. Externally it is used on
slow-healing cuts and burns.

Parts used: Usually the fresh flowers, but dried flowers can also be
used.

A compact deciduous tree, often with straight sharp thorns, and dense white hairs on young shoots and leaves. The broad, shallowly-lobed leaves have serrated margins. White five-petalled flowers grow in spreading clusters in spring and are followed by clusters of scarlet, rounded berries in fall.

Found along streams, in bottomlands and open woods from Nova Scotia to North Dakota and south to Alabama and Texas.

Heart tonic, astringent, diuretic, sedative. Tea made from the flowers, taken over a period of weeks, can be used to regulate heart action and lower blood pressure; it also aids sleep. The liquid obtained from boiling the fruits has the same effects, and is also used to treat kidney problems and sore throats.

Parts used: dried flowers, fresh or dried fruits. Fruits can be made into jam. There are many Hawthorn species with flowers and fruits which can be used in this way.

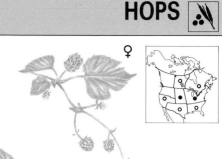

A climbing perennial plant, with twining stems which twist clockwise. Large, opposite leaves have three to five palmate lobes and toothed margins. Male and female flowers grow on separate plants. Female flowers are like small cones; they enlarge to become pale yellow-green "hops" with papery bracts.

Cultivated for use in beer making and also found wild in woods from Nova Scotia to Manitoba and Montana, south to North Carolina and Arizona. Grown in California.

Sedative, relieves pain, diuretic. An infusion can be used to alleviate insomnia and calm nerves, also to improve digestion and settle a nervous stomach. It is a good tonic for stomach and liver. Externally, it can be used with poppies to treat neuralgia, inflamed or rheumatic joints and boils.

Parts used; female flowers and dried "hops" or fruits. Hop fruits are an essential ingredient of beer. Young tips and leaves can be used as a green vegetable.

79

Shrubs with arching spiny or thorny branches and alternate compound leaves. The leaves have three to nine leaflets, depending on species. Flowers are large and conspicuous, pink or rose colored, with five petals and many stamens. Fruits are smooth, fleshy red hips containing hairs and seeds.

Found in open woods and woodland edges, in hedgerows and old pastures, on roadsides, dunes and along rivers. About 35 species distributed throughout the USA and Canada.

Mildly astringent and diuretic, carminative. Hips contain Vitamin C in large amounts, also Vitamin A, iron and phosphorus. An infusion or syrup made from the hips can be used to treat colds, as a spring tonic and to combat scurvy. It is also used to treat diarrhea and stomach cramps.

Parts used: hips, with seeds and hairs removed. Leaves can be used to make tea. All roses, like **Carolina Rose** illustrated, have edible hips, but they vary in size and quality.

COMMON JUNIPER

1–4ft

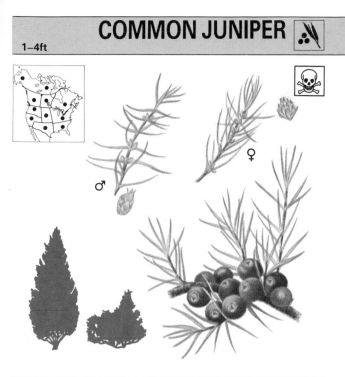

An evergreen, usually low-spreading or prostrate conifer, with brown, shredding bark. Leaves sharp-pointed, with a white band on their upper surface; they grow in whorls of three. Globular fruits are small, fleshy, berry-like cones, green at first, turning blue-black with a white bloom, in the second year.

Found in dry rocky soils (and the prostrate form on coastal dunes) throughout North America.

Diuretic, digestive, antiseptic, rubefacient, tonic, carminative. Usually eaten as fresh berries or made into a tea to aid digestion and relieve flatulence. Also used to treat dropsy and kidney disorders, but large doses may irritate the kidneys. Can also relieve rheumatism.

Parts used: berries, either fresh or dried. They are not only used in herb medicine, but also to flavor meats, in making sauerkraut and to give its distinctive flavor to gin.

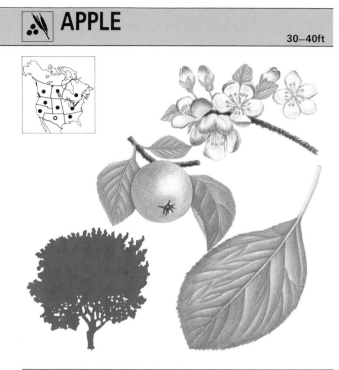

A small deciduous tree with a dense crown and gray bark. The twigs are downy at first. Toothed, elliptical pointed leaves grow with pink-flushed, white flowers on short side twigs. Flowers open with the leaves. Fruits are rounded green apples, depressed at each end, flushing red in fall.

Cultivated throughout much of North America and naturalized in eastern USA, on the prairies, in southern Canada and the Pacific states.

Astringent, laxative, diuretic. Apples regulate the digestive system, preventing constipation and stopping diarrhea; they also help to neutralize the effects of rich fatty foods. They help to purify the blood, clear gout and rheumatism, and prevent gallstones. They also help to keep the teeth clean.

Parts used: ripe fruits, raw or cooked. Wild apples are quite often hybrids between the Cultivated Apple and the native Crab-apple species.

1–2ft

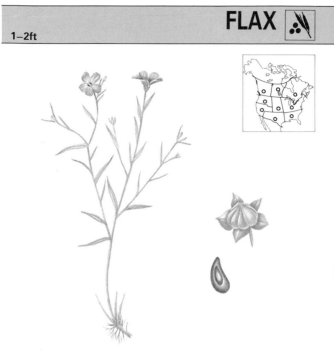

An annual plant with a single leafy stem, branching near the top to form an inflorescence. The numerous leaves are alternate, stalkless, linear with three parallel nerves. Flowers are delicate and bright blue with five petals. Fruits are capsules with small, polished brown, oval beaked seeds.

Found on roadsides, in waste places and old fields where it has escaped from cultivation throughout the USA and Canada. Native to Europe.

Emollient, demulcent, laxative. Bruised seeds swell up in the intestines and stimulate bowel action, relieving constipation. Linseed oil poultices are used to treat rheumatism and other inflammations. The oil is also used in cough medicines and to treat dyspepsia, gastritis and to remove gallstones.

Parts used: ripe seeds. Linseed oil is obtained from the crushed seeds. Flax is also grown for the linen fibers which are obtained from the stems.

1–3ft

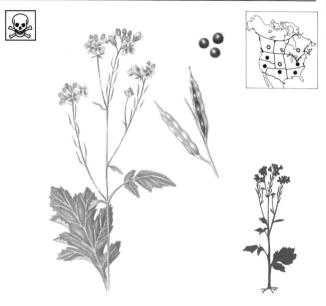

An annual plant with many erect branched stems. Lower leaves are large, lobed and bristly, upper ones smaller, toothed and hairless. Bright yellow flowers grow in elongating clusters terminating stems; each has four petals. Fruits are upright, beaked pods, held on stalks close to flower stalks.

Found in fields and waste places, as an escape from cultivation and often naturalized. Throughout the USA and in the eastern and Pacific areas of southern Canada.

Stimulant, irritant, emetic, digestive. Chiefly used to draw blood from one place to another, in poultices to treat colds, bronchitis, rheumatism, chilblains etc. Can also be used to stimulate digestion, to relieve constipation or to promote kidney action. In stronger doses it causes vomiting.

Parts used: seeds. Mustard must be used in small quantities and for short periods, otherwise it causes irritation and inflammation. White Mustard seeds are less powerful.

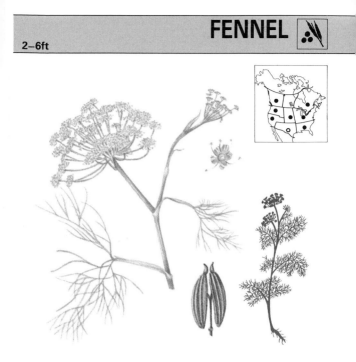

A stout, strongly scented perennial plant, with erect stems and blue-green feathery leaves. The striated stems are solid when young, becoming hollow with age. The yellow flowers grow in compound, terminal umbels, each with 10–30 stalks. Aniseed-scented, egg-shaped fruits follow the flowers.

Found growing as a weed in waste places in much of the USA, in southeastern Canada and in southern B.C. Also cultivated. Native to Mediterranean Europe.

Antispasmodic, carminative, diuretic, expectorant, aids digestion, promotes lactation. An infusion can be used to stimulate appetite, dispel wind and alleviate intestinal cramps; also as a remedy for sore throats and coughs. It can also be used to bathe sore eyes.

Parts used: fruits. One of the constituents of gripe water, with Dill and Anise, also in cough medicines. Fennel leaves may be cooked in sauces for oily fish or used in salads.

CARAWAY

1–2ft

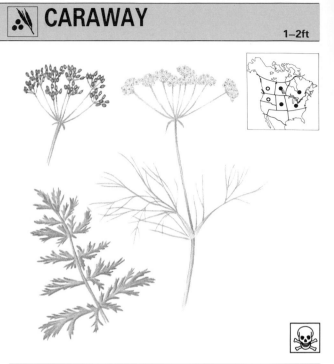

A biennial plant, with a rosette of ferny leaves in the first year and a hollow, branched, leafy flowering stem in the second. White flowers grow in compound umbels, with 5–12 very unequal stalks; outer flowers larger than inner ones. Fruits are oblong with low ridges, strongly scented when rubbed.

Cultivated and found growing as a weed in waste places from Newfoundland to Alberta and south to Pennsylvania and Colorado. Native to Eurasia.

Antispasmodic, carminative, stimulates appetite and digestion. An infusion of caraway seeds or a handful of chewed seeds can be used as a remedy for indigestion and wind. The infusion may be given to children and infants for colic. It is also used to alleviate menstrual cramps.

Parts used: fruits. Also used as a flavoring in cooking. It is best grown in the garden rather than gathered wild, because of its resemblance to poisonous relatives, like Poison Hemlock.

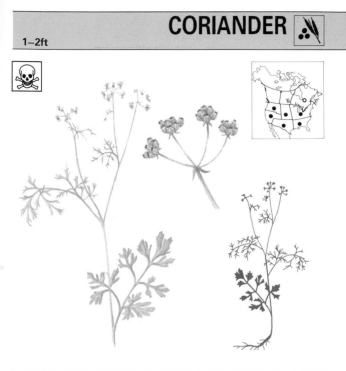

1–2ft

An erect, shining annual with an unpleasant scent. It has pinnate leaves, the lower ones with oval leaflets, upper ones with narrow ones. White flowers are borne in compound umbels, each made up of 3–5 small umbels. Red-brown fruits are hard and egg-shaped, borne in pairs which do not separate.

Cultivated and grows as a weed in much of the USA, especially in eastern and southern areas. Native to Mediterranean Europe.

Stimulant, carminative, antispasmodic. Coriander fruits stimulate the appetite, aid digestion and dispel wind; they can also be used to treat diarrhea and colic. Coriander may be added to herb medicines, to give a pleasant flavor.

Parts used: fruits. Also used to flavor bread and liqueurs and in curry powder. It is safer to use cultivated plants, since wild plants may be mistaken for poisonous relatives.

A densely branched, deciduous shrub, with many tripartite spines on the yellowish branches. The oval, finely toothed leaves grow crowded together on short shoots. Drooping clusters of yellow flowers are followed by clusters of oblong, orange-red berries in late summer and fall.

Introduced from Europe, this shrub is widely planted in northeastern USA, where it has become naturalized in fence rows and on roadsides, in waste ground and disturbed woods.

Tonic, digestive, laxative. An infusion of bark can be used to stimulate liver action, and in the treatment of jaundice and dyspepsia. In larger doses it acts as a laxative but should be used in moderation. Tea made from twigs and dried fruits contains Vitamin C and can be taken to combat exhaustion.

Parts used: dried bark of stems or roots; twigs and dried berries. The berries can also be made into jellies or cooked with other fruits.

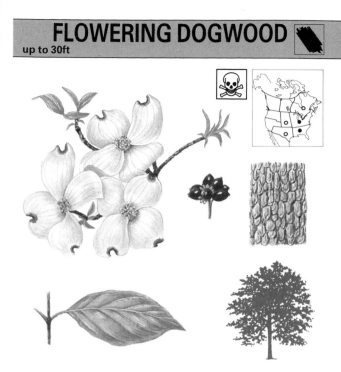

FLOWERING DOGWOOD

up to 30ft

A tree with a short trunk and wide, nearly horizontal branches. The leaves are opposite, elliptical, with wavy margins. The tiny flowers grow in clusters of 20–30, each cluster bordered by four wide, white, petal-like bracts. Fruits are shiny red, elliptical berries, borne in clusters.

Found in the understorey of woods, along roadsides and in old fields, from Maine to southern Ontario, and south to Florida and Texas.

Astringent, stimulant, tonic, reduces fever. Liquid obtained from boiling the bark was traditionally used by Indians to treat intermittent fevers, like malaria. It can also be used in an ointment for sores and ulcers.

Parts used: dried bark. Fresh bark upsets the stomach and bowels. Other Dogwood species also have medicinal properties.

up to 70ft

A deciduous tree with gray bark fissured to expose inner reddish bark. The alternate leaves are shiny dark green, elliptical with saw-toothed margins. White flowers are borne in dense drooping spikes. Fruits are strings of small, juicy cherries, dark red turning black.

Found in woods and thickets from Nova Scotia to Florida and west to Minnesota and Texas. Also planted in towns and cities.

Astringent, sedative, aids digestion. An infusion of the dried bark is a traditional remedy for coughs and for treating bronchitis, colds and catarrh. Also used to treat dyspepsia. Used by American Indians as a pain reliever and to treat diarrhea.

Parts used: dried inner bark. Leaves and seeds are poisonous. The fruits of the related Wild Plum are laxative.

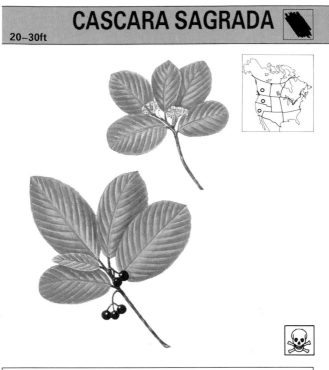

A large, deciduous shrub or small tree with thinly fissured gray bark. It has many upright branches which bear terminal tufts of broadly elliptical, wavy-edged leaves. Clusters of small greenish, bell-shaped flowers grow in the leaf axils; they are followed by juicy berries, purplish black when ripe.

Found in moist places, in the understorey of coniferous forests, along roadsides from B.C. to California. Also below 5000ft. in the Rocky Mountains, south to Idaho and Montana.

Laxative, stimulates appetite. An infusion of the dried bark is one of the best laxatives for chronic constipation since it tones up the bowels. Also used as a remedy for dyspepsia and as a treatment for liver and gallbladder problems. It regularizes the digestive system and gets it working again.

Parts used: inner bark, dried for one to three years before use. Fresh bark is emetic. The European Alder Buckthorn, grown in the east, has similar uses but is not as mild.

A large thicket-forming shrub with prickly stems and aromatic leaves. The large, compound leaves are dull green with 5–11 oblong leaflets. Clusters of tiny yellow-green flowers, male and female on separate plants, are followed by small pod-like brown fruits, splitting open to reveal the "berries."

Found in moist and rocky woods, and on river banks from southern Quebec and Ontario south to Georgia and Oklahoma, but much less common in the south.

Stimulant, relieves pain, promotes sweating. An infusion of dried bark or berries may be taken to improve the blood circulation and to treat rheumatism. As a wash, an infusion of powdered bark may be used to cleanse old wounds and ulcers. Fresh bark may be chewed to alleviate toothache.

Parts used: dried powdered bark and berries. Southern Prickly Ash or Hercules-club is a related shrub which can be used in similar ways; it has shiny leaves and spiny knobs on its bark.

up to 20ft

A tall shrub with smooth light brown bark and spreading branches. It has broadly oval leaves with wavy margins. The few yellow flowers have linear twisted petals and grow on barc branches in fall and winter. Fruits are hard, light brown capsules with four points, maturing the following fall.

Found in the understorey of moist deciduous woods from Quebec and Nova Scotia to Minnesota and south to Florida and Texas.

Astringent, sedative, tonic, stops bleeding. The liquid from boiling bark or leaves in water can be used as a gargle for throat irritations, as a vaginal douche or to douche piles. In a poultice or bandage, it stops bleeding from varicose veins, is used for treating bruises, insect bites and poison ivy.

Parts used: bark and leaves. A distillation of Witch Hazel in alcohol is widely available and is used to bathe bruises, stings and burns.

A deciduous tree, with up to four leaning trunks, ascending branches and furrowed, dark brown bark. Leaves are narrow and finely toothed, 3–5in. long, often curved to one side, shiny green on upper surface, paler below. Male catkins are yellow, females green, appearing with the leaves on separate trees.

Found beside streams, rivers and ditches, beside lakes and in wet meadows. From New Brunswick to Minnesota, south to Florida and Texas; also, less commonly, west from Texas to California.

Astringent, reduces fever, relieves pain, diuretic. The bark contains salicin, which has similar effects to aspirin. The liquid obtained from boiling the bark kills pain of headaches, rheumatism and arthritis, brings down fever of colds and flu, reduces inflammation. It is a good wash for sores and burns.

Parts used: dried bark. Bark from other willows, like the White Willow, introduced from Europe in the east, can be used in the same ways.

A large tree with dark gray-brown bark. It has long-stalked, opposite, palmate leaves with 5–7 leaflets. Flowers are borne in showy, pyramidal clusters in early summer; each flower has four white petals, with a basal yellow spot on each. Round, green, spiny fruits enclose 1–3 brown shiny seeds.

This tree has been extensively planted as a street tree in cities in many parts of the USA and Canada. Native to southeastern Europe.

Astringent, expectorant. An infusion from the bark reduces fever and can be used as a remedy for bronchitis and inflammations of the stomach. Externally it is used to treat leg ulcers, varicose veins and piles. The chopped seeds have been used to treat bronchitis and rheumatism.

Parts used: bark, stripped in spring and dried in sun. The leaves, fruits and seeds are poisonous in large quantities.

A tree with a broad crown and deeply furrowed, dark brown bark. The thick, stiff leaves are 4–8in. long, with rough upper sides and hairy beneath; they have doubly serrated margins and unequal sides. Dark red spring flowers are followed by almost round, flattened, light green fruits, each with one seed.

Found in moist woods in the eastern USA and Canada except the extreme south, north to Quebec and west to Texas and Kansas. Also widely planted as a street tree in these areas.

Demulcent, emollient, diuretic. Slippery elm food is made like custard with powdered bark and soothes sore throats, coughs, stomach and intestinal inflammations, diarrhea, inflamed kidneys. It is an excellent food for convalescents. It can also be used in poultices for skin irritations and wounds.

Parts used: dried, powdered inner bark. This is white and mucilaginous when fresh. Whole trees are stripped of their bark for commercial use, when the tree dies.

A large tree with widespread branches and light gray, fissured bark. The alternate, deciduous leaves are bright green and hairless, widest beyond the middle, with 3–5 pairs of rounded lobes. Light brown, ovoid acorns grow on current year's twigs in bowl-shaped cups enclosing a quarter of the acorn.

Found in upland woods throughout eastern USA from Maine to Minnesota and south to Florida and Texas; north into the extreme southern areas of Ontario and Quebec.

Astringent, tonic. An infusion of bark can be used to reduce heavy periods. It is used as a gargle for mouth and throat infections and externally to treat vaginal problems and piles. As a wash, it is used for bathing skin irritations and sore eyes, to stop bleeding from cuts and to treat varicose veins.

Parts used: dried powdered bark from the branches. The bark of Red Oak can be used externally as a wash.

97

SWEET GUM

60–100ft

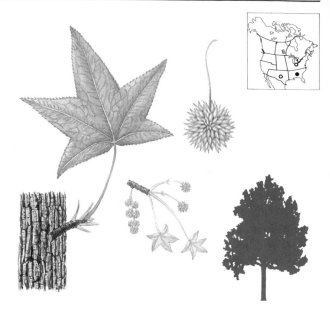

A large tree with a conical crown and deeply furrowed gray bark. Its leaves are star-shaped, usually with 5–7 toothed lobes and an aromatic scent when crushed. The flowers are borne in green balls, male and female in separate clusters on the same tree. Fruits are spiky brown hanging balls.

Found in mixed woods, in moist soils; also planted in cities in the east, in the Pacific states and B.C. Native from southern Connecticut south to Florida and west to Texas.

Astringent, expectorant, antiseptic. The balsam can be made into an antiseptic ointment for treating wounds and skin inflammations. An infusion or syrup made from the bark or the balsam can be used to treat coughs and colds, also to treat diarrhea and dysentery.

Parts used: balsam (the resin that is exuded by the bark.)

BASSWOOD

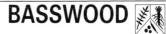

A large tree with dark gray, furrowed bark, older trees with sprouts around the base of the trunk. The broad, rounded leaves, 3–6in. long, have pointed tips and heart-shaped bases. Clusters of yellow-white fragrant flowers grow on long stalks from narrow bracts; they are followed by small round nutlets.

Found in moist soil, in woods and forests, in uplands and valleys from Quebec to North Dakota and south to North Carolina and Oklahoma. Also planted in cities in this area.

Emollient, digestive, promotes sweating. An infusion of the flowers and leaves is used as a sedative and is a traditional remedy for sore throats, colds and flu. The bark is emollient and, beaten into a pulp with water, makes a good dressing for wounds, sores and burns.

Parts used: bark, and leaves and flowers, dried in shade. Also known as American Linden. Other Lindens, like the commonly planted European Linden, can be used in the same way.

up to 30ft

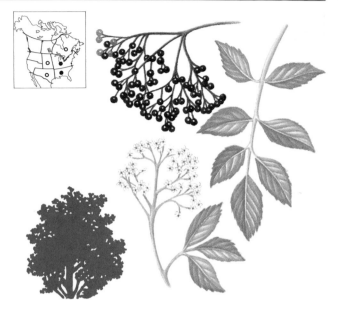

A broad shrub with stout, rather soft, pithy, arching branches and stout twigs. The dark green leaves are opposite and compound, usually with 5–11 lance-shaped leaflets. Creamy white, scented flowers grow in flat clusters and are followed by large, flat clusters of small, purple-black, juicy berries.

Found in damp rich soils, in woods and thickets, along trails and roadsides, woodland margins, fences and ditches, in fields, in the USA east of the Rockies and in southeastern Canada.

Diuretic, emetic, purgative, promotes sweating. An ointment made from the leaves can be used to treat bruises and sprains. An infusion of the flowers induces sweating and can be used to treat colds and flu. Berries can be cooked into juice or made into syrup; both are good cold treatments and laxatives.

Parts used: leaves, flowers and berries. Elderflower water can be used as a skin cleanser. Both flowers and berries are made into wines. Berries are also made into jam.

SMOOTH SUMAC

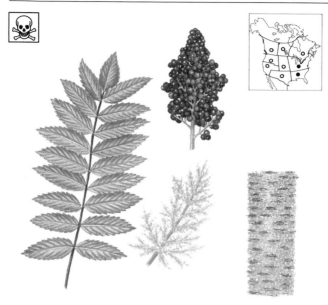

A small tree or large shrub with thick branches and smooth gray bark. It has large, deciduous, compound leaves with 11–31 saw-toothed, hairless leaflets. Dense cone-shaped clusters of whitish male and female flowers grow on separate plants. Fruits are dark red, fuzzy berries in similar dense clusters.

Found along roadsides and in waste land, abandoned fields and grasslands, woodland margins and clearings. Eastern USA, into southern Canada and west to the prairies. Also in the Rockies.

Bark and leaves are astringent, antiseptic and tonic. Fruits are diuretic and cooling. Tea made from bark or leaves can be used to treat sore throats and diarrhea. Tea made from leaves and berries can be used for kidney and bladder problems. Fresh fruits are cooling and fruit tea is a gargle for mouth ulcers.

Parts used: leaves, bark, fruit. Staghorn Sumac can be used in the same way. Careful identification is essential, since sumacs with smooth white berries (like Poison Oak) are poisonous.

A tree with chalky white, papery bark, peeling in strips. Leaves are rounded-triangular with toothed margins. Yellowish male and gray-green female catkins appear in winter, enlarging in spring when males turn yellow with pollen. Green female catkins enlarge to produce numerous two-winged seeds.

Found in upland woods, often in pure stands, from Labrador to Alaska, near the northern limit for trees, south to North Carolina and Colorado, in mountains in the south of its range.

Diuretic, promotes sweating, astringent. An infusion made with leaves stimulates kidneys and can be used to help dispel gravel; also to soothe rheumatism and arthritis. Liquid from boiling bark can be used to wash sores and wounds. Sap can be taken as a spring tonic or used as a hair tonic.

Parts used: leaves, fresh or dried; inner bark; sap in spring. An infusion made from the twigs of Yellow Birch or Sweet Birch is a folk remedy for headaches, colds, rheumatism and lumbago.

BLACKCURRANT

A small deciduous shrub. The large, strongly scented leaves are broader than long and have three to five lobes. The green, bell-shaped flowers grow in drooping sprays in the leaf axils and are followed by drooping sprays of black, juicy, round berries.

This is the Garden Blackcurrant, native to Europe and cultivated in North America. Two closely related native blackcurrants grow in wet woods in Canada and northern USA.

Diuretic, anti-inflammatory, promotes sweating. Fruits contain Vitamin C. Juice from berries is useful in treating diarrhea, stomach cramps and for stimulating the kidneys. Leaf tea aids kidney function and is useful in rheumatism and gout. Tea made with berries makes a good mouthwash for bleeding gums.

Parts used: dried leaves, fresh or dried fruits. Fruits can be made into cordials or jams. Redcurrants and the fruits of the wild Golden Currants are also rich in Vitamin C.

RED RASPBERRY

up to 6ft

Spreading or trailing, very prickly shrub with stiff hairs on the often white-powdered stems. The compound leaves have three to seven leaflets, pale green to whitish and hairy on the underside. Small clusters of greenish white flowers are followed by bright red, many-sectioned, globular fruits.

Found on woodland margins and in clearings, on roadsides and in old fields across southern Canada, into northeastern USA and south through the Rocky Mountains.

Astringent, stimulant. Raspberry leaf tea can be used to alleviate period pains, and as a remedy for diarrhea and stomach upsets. It also makes a good gargle for a sore mouth and can be used as a wash for sores and ulcers. The fruits are cooling and mildly laxative.

Parts used: leaves and fruits. Other species have similarly edible fruits. The roots of Whitebark Raspberry can be pulped and used as a dressing for rheumatic pain, bruises and burns.

BLACKBERRY

up to 10ft

A shrub with erect stems bearing many straight prickles and alternate compound leaves. The leaves usually have five rounded leaflets, and there are hooked prickles on the veins and stalks. Long clusters of white five-petalled flowers are followed by sweet, juicy, black, many-sectioned fruits.

Found in woods and along woodland edges, in hedgerows, along roadsides and on disturbed ground. Northeastern USA, west into Minnesota and south to Tennessee.

Astringent, tonic. An infusion of the leaves can be used to treat diarrhea and stomach upset. The liquid from boiling the roots in water can be used in the same way, and is stronger; it can also be used to combat dropsy. Blackberry fruits are effective against diarrhea.

Parts used: roots, leaves and fruits. Other species of blackberries can be used in the same ways.

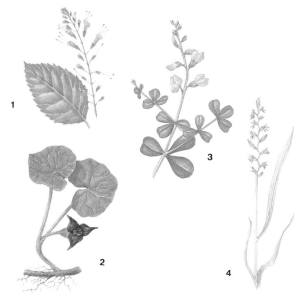

Stone Root (1)
Perennial with four-sided stems, up to 4ft. tall, & pointed-oval opposite leaves. Flowers yellow, lemon-scented & two-lipped with fringed lower lip. Rich woods, E. USA & Can. Tea made with fresh rhizome makes good diuretic.

Wild Ginger (2)
Pairs of large, heart-shaped leaves grow from creeping rhizomes. Tiny tubular red-brown flowers grow at base of leafstalks. Eastern woods. Tea made with dried rhizome used to treat upset stomach & wind, & to stimulate appetite.

Wild Indigo (3)
Perennial bushy plant, up to 3ft. tall, with small clover-like leaves & many terminal clusters of yellow pea-like flowers. Dry soil. E. USA & Can. Infusion of the rhizome can be used as antiseptic wash for ulcers, sores & wounds.

Quack Grass (4)
Spreading grass with many thin rhizomes & thin green leaves. Long narrow flower spikes have many spikelets. Weed of waste places. Much of N. Amer. Infusion of rhizome used to treat catarrh, rheumatism, kidney gravel.

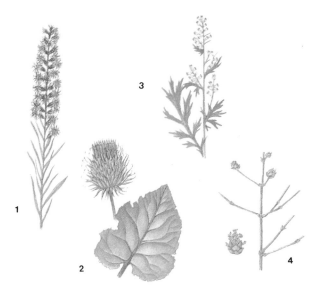

Marsh Blazing Star (1)
Erect stem, 2–6ft. tall, bears
many linear leaves & dense
terminal spikes of purple flower
heads. Wet places. E. USA.
Liquid obtained from boiling
roots can be used as a gargle for
sore throat. Rough Blazing Star
used in same way.

Common Burdock (2)
Large biennial plant with
reddish stems & heart-shaped
leaves in second year. Bracts
from red-purple flower heads
form burrs. Waste places. S.
Can. & USA. Roots are boiled &
liquid used as wash for skin
problems, boils, rheumatism.

Mugwort (3)
Aromatic plant with reddish,
erect stems. Divided leaves are
dark green above, whitish
beneath. Many small reddish-
brown flower heads have
cobwebby bracts. Waste places.
E. USA & E. Can. Infusion of
dried plant stimulates digestion.

Mormon Tea (4)
Branched shrub, with jointed
green stems, up to 6ft. tall. Two
or three scale-like leaves grow at
each node. Male and female
cones grow on separate plants.
S.W. deserts. Anti-spasmodic.
Tea made from stems is used as
remedy for asthma.

OTHER USEFUL PLANTS

Yerba Santa (1)
Aromatic shrub with erect stems, up to 10ft. high, thick lance-shaped leaves & terminal clusters of lavender flowers. Chaparral, foothills of Sierra Nevada. Expectorant, lowers fever. Tea made with leaves is old remedy for colds & flu.

Turtlehead (2)
Erect stems, up to 3ft. tall, with opposite, lance-shaped leaves & terminal spikes of white, swollen, two-lipped flowers. Wet eastern woods. Tea made with fresh leaves can be used for liver disorders & dyspepsia; also a vermifuge.

Liverleaf (3)
Small perennial plant with clump of rounded, three-lobed leaves & solitary pink, blue or white flowers. Woods. E. USA & Canada. Infusion of leaves can be used to soothe liver problems, coughs and chest diseases.

Coltsfoot (4)
Perennial plant with yellow flower heads on purplish scaly stems in spring, then rosettes of large heart-shaped leaves. Waste places. N.E. USA & E. Can. Infusion of leaves is remedy for coughs & bronchitis. Often used in cough medicines.

Common Storksbill (1)
Small plant with lacy leaves, small clusters of flowers on long stalks & fruits like storks' bills. Fields, waste places. E. USA & Can. Stops bleeding. An infusion of leaves can be used to stop excessive menstruation.

Evening Primrose (2)
Biennial plant, with tall flowering spike in second year. Large yellow flowers are followed by erect capsules. Fields, prairies, roadsides. Much of USA & S. Can. Infusion of leaves is astringent, soothing.

American Pennyroyal (3)
Annual, hairy aromatic mint with small opposite leaves & blue-violet, two-lipped flowers in leaf axils. Dry woods & fields. N.E. USA. Tea made with flowering tops is old remedy for wind & nausea, also for menstrual cramps.

American Mountain Ash (4)
Large deciduous shrub with compound leaves, large clusters of white flowers & clusters of orange-red berries. Moist soils. E. USA & Can. An infusion of dried flowers is diuretic & a mild laxative, as are berries.

109

OTHER USEFUL PLANTS

Dill (1)
Aromatic annual plant with hollow stems, feathery leaves & umbels of small yellow flowers. Seeds are elliptical, flattened. Waste places. Most of USA. Seeds are carminative, antispasmodic. Used to relieve flatulence & upset stomach.

Bilberry (2)
Creeping shrub, with green branched stems, oval leaves & bell-shaped flowers. Berries are round, blue-black, juicy. Mountain woods. W. Can. & USA. Berries contain Vitamin C & can be used to treat diarrhea & to regulate intestines.

Prickly Lettuce (3)
Erect stem has lobed or lance-shaped prickly leaves & many yellow flower heads. Plant filled with milky juice. Waste places. Most of USA & southern Can. Dried juice has been used to calm nerves, induce sleep & soothe coughs.

Eucalyptus (4)
Tall tree with evergreen, curved, lance-shaped leaves. Flowers have no petals & many white stamens. Fruits bluish, top-shaped capsules. Calif. Eucalyptus oil made into cough drops & asthma inhalants. Also used as a bath additive.

110

Quaking Aspen (1)

Deciduous tree, up to 100ft. tall, with heart-shaped leaves that shiver constantly. Upland woods & cutover land. Throughout N. Amer. Bark has similar effects to willow bark. Infusion is used to treat coughs & colds, & as a wash for wounds.

Black Walnut (2)

Large open tree with dark, ridged bark. Aromatic compound leaves have 9–21 leaflets. Walnuts have rough husks. Moist soils. E. USA & Can. Infusion of bark can be used to stop diarrhea or as a mouthwash.

Fringe Tree (3)

Shrub, up to 30ft. tall, with opposite, elliptical leaves & drooping clusters of fragrant flowers. Each flower has four narrow petals. Moist woods & streamsides. S.E. USA. Infusion of bark can be used to treat liver problems & reduce fever.

Highbush Cranberry (4)

Shrub, up to 12ft. tall, with three-lobed leaves. Flower clusters have inner fertile flowers, outer sterile ones. Fruits are red berries. Moist woods. Much of N. Amer. Infusion of bark used to combat menstrual & other cramps.

A large, unpleasantly scented, perennial plant with a clump of large compound leaves. The leaflets are coarsely toothed and borne in threes. Flowers grow in long slender, "fluffy" spikes terminating tall leafy stalks; each flower has numerous white stamens and no petals. Fruits are pods with several seeds.

Found in rich woodland from southern Ontario to Massachusetts and south to Georgia and Tennessee.

Astringent, diuretic, expectorant, antispasmodic, sedative. The liquid obtained from boiling the roots can be used to treat whooping cough, bronchitis and other coughs. In small doses it is used to treat diarrhea in children. It has also been used to alleviate rheumatism.

Parts used: dried roots. This plant must only be used in small quantities since strong doses cause nausea and vomiting.

SENEGA SNAKEROOT

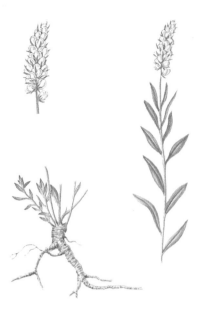

A perennial plant with unbranched, leafy, upright stems growing from a woody crown. Each stem bears many alternate, lance-shaped, almost stalkless leaves and a dense terminal spike of flowers. The flowers are pea-like, white or greenish white in color.

Found in dry, often rocky woods and prairies, on hillsides in Canada from Newfoundland to Alberta and south in the USA from the Dakotas and New England to Arkansas and Georgia.

Stimulant, expectorant, diuretic, promotes sweating; emetic in strong doses. An infusion of the dried root is most commonly used as an expectorant in coughs, asthma and bronchitis. It can also be used in whooping cough and rheumatism.

Parts used: dried root. Too strong a dose causes vomiting and diarrhea and an overdose is poisonous. No more than one cup of the infusion should be drunk in a day.

🕱 BUTTERFLY WEED

1

A hairy, perennial plant with a large tuber-like root and an erect, branched, leafy stem. Leaves are long and narrow with watery sap. Flowers are bright orange, stamens forming a structure like a crown, with five turned-back petals; they grow in terminal umbels. Seed pods are spindle-shaped.

Found in fields and woods, in meadows and prairies, on roadsides, often in dry sandy soil. From Newfoundland to Ontario, south to Florida and Arizona.

Expectorant, antispasmodic, carminative, promotes sweating. Used by American Indians and in later herb medicine to treat bronchitis, pleurisy, flu and other chest infections as well as colds. Also used in treatment of diarrhea and dysentery, and of rheumatism.

Parts used: dried roots. Also known as Pleurisy Root. Poisonous in large doses. The related **Common Milkweed (1)** has been used as a diuretic, but is much more poisonous.

A perennial hairy plant with a knotted yellow rhizome. It has one long-stalked basal leaf and a single stem with two leaves near the top; leaves are large, wrinkled and palmately cleft. Solitary terminal flower has three whitish sepals which soon fall and many stamens. Fruit is head of small red berries.

Originally found in rich woods from Vermont to Minnesota and south to Georgia and Arkansas, as far west as Nebraska. Now rare or extinct in many places due to overcollecting.

Antiseptic, astringent, tonic, laxative, stops bleeding. In modern medicine the fluid extract is used to treat catarrhal and digestive disorders. An infusion can be used as an eyewash, as a mouthwash, to treat skin irritations, infections and sores, as a vaginal douche and to treat piles.

Parts used: dried rhizome. An important plant in the herb medicine of many American Indians; they also used it as a dye. In large doses Goldenseal is very poisonous.

115

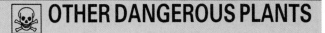

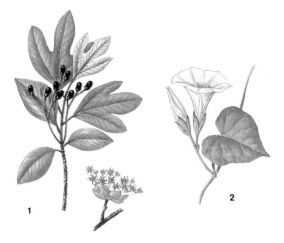

Sassafras (1)
Small tree with green twigs &
large simple or lobed leaves.
Leaves have spicy odor when
crushed. Yellow flowers appear
on twigs before leaves & are
followed by dark, shiny blue
berries. Woods & lower slopes in
E. USA. Hot infusion of dried
root bark has been used to treat
rheumatism, arthritis & gout; &
as a wash for skin irritations &
ulcers. Doubt has arisen as to its
safety since it is thought to
contain potential carcinogens.

Jalap (2)
Perennial hairless vine with large
tuber-like roots & trailing stems.
Leaves are pointed heart-
shaped, alternate. Flowers large
& funnel-shaped, white with
purple centers, in clusters on
long stalks in leaf axils. Woods
in eastern USA. Cathartic,
purgative. Dried roots are
usually mixed in small quantities
with other plants like rhubarb,
in laxatives. Too strong a dose
causes purging & vomiting.

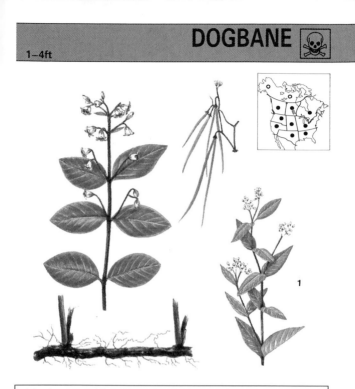

A bushy perennial, hairless plant with tough fibrous bark on the stems, exuding milky juice when broken. Leaves are smooth and oblong, opposite and drooping. Nodding bell-shaped flowers are fragrant, pink with red markings inside; borne in terminal clusters and in upper leaf axils. Fruits are slender pods.

Found in dry woodland, also less commonly on roadsides and in fields, from Newfoundland to B.C., south to Georgia and Arizona.

Diuretic, emetic, cathartic. Used to reduce dropsy after heart failure and in the treatment of liver disorders and gallstones. Also used to relieve dyspepsia and constipation. Has a beneficial effect in treatment of rheumatism. Larger doses cause vomiting and may cause other symptoms of poisoning.

Parts used: dried rhizome. Not to be used without medical supervision. **Hemp Dogbane (1)** is used in medicine in the treatment of heart failure but even small doses are dangerous.

8–18in

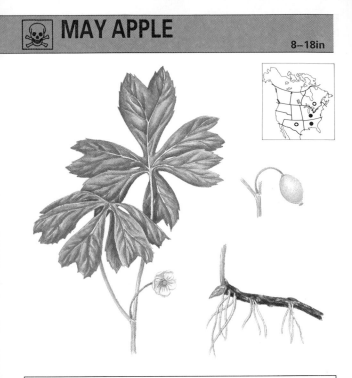

A perennial plant with thick jointed tubers and dense patches of upright stems, each with one or two large, deeply divided, umbrella-like leaves. A leaf may measure up to 14in. across. Stems with two leaves also bear a single nodding, white waxy flower, followed by an egg-shaped, greenish yellow berry.

Found in rich moist deciduous woods and on shady roadsides, in clearings and meadows. Eastern USA and Canada, from southern Quebec and Minnesota to Florida and Texas.

Expectorant, purgative, cathartic. The drug is used in the treatment of liver disorders, stimulating liver and intestinal action. Also used as a powerful laxative and in the treatment of some cancers. In very small quantities it is used in the treatment of skin diseases.

Parts used: dried tubers. A powerful poisonous drug, only used with medical supervision. The pulp of the berry is edible, all other parts of the plant, including the seeds, are poisonous.

INDIAN TOBACCO

1–2ft

An annual plant with an erect, often branched stem. Leaves are alternate, stalkless, oval with serrated margins. Solitary violet or white flowers grow in upper leaf axils; each is two-lipped, with the two-lobed upper lip erect and the three-lobed lower lip spreading. Fruits are capsules in swollen calyces.

Found in fields and woods, as a weed in yards and on roadsides. Across southern Canada from the east coast to Saskatchewan, south to Georgia, Kansas and Arkansas.

Expectorant, antispasmodic, promotes sweating. Has been used in treatment of asthma, bronchitis and whooping cough, also of epilepsy and illnesses which result in convulsions. In ointments, it has been used on sprains, bruises and skin diseases. Dry leaves have been used as tobacco (hence Indian Tobacco.)

Parts used: dried whole plant and seeds. Poisonous. Overdose can lead to nausea, cold sweats, paralysis and possibly death.

Virginia Snakeroot (1)
Perennial plant with a short horizontal rhizome & an erect crooked stem, 1–3ft. tall, with a few alternate pointed heart-shaped leaves. Solitary flowers grow very near the base of the stem; they are purplish, S-shaped with an expanded tip & have a foul scent. Woodland. E. USA. Stimulant, bitter tonic, promotes sweating. Used in small quantities, a cold infusion of dried rhizome stimulates the appetite & aids digestion but too large a dose causes nausea, vomiting & diarrhea.

Pokeweed (2)
Clump-forming perennial plant, up to 9ft. tall, with a disagreeable scent. It has several reddish, branched stems & many large, lance-shaped leaves. Long drooping sprays of white flowers are followed by sprays of purple-black berries. Disturbed places. S. Can., E. & S. USA. Purgative, emetic, relieves pain. Leaves & roots have been used to treat rheumatism & arthritis, also in treatment of piles & as a laxative. Has been used in treatment of some cancers. Poisonous.

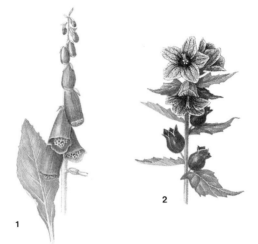

Foxglove (1)
Biennial plant with a rosette of leaves in the first year, a leafy erect flowering stem in the second. Leaves are large & softly hairy, ovate or lance-shaped with winged stalks. Large bell-shaped, purple flowers have spotted insides; they are borne in a tall spike. Cultivated & escaped in E. and W. Shady places. The drug digitalin is extracted from the leaves. It is used to regularize & slow heart beat & increase blood pressure. It is also a powerful diuretic. Digitalin is a deadly poison.

Henbane (2)
A sticky fetid annual or biennial plant with an erect stem & deeply toothed leaves. Clusters of yellow, purple-veined, bell-shaped flowers grow in the upper leaf axils. Waste places & roadsides. S. Can. & N. USA. Contains the narcotics, hyoscyamine & scopolamine, which are used as pain killers & to induce sleep. Also antispasmodic in its action, it is used as a muscle relaxant & in the treatment of asthma. Deadly poisonous.

121

Index and check-list

All species in Roman type are illustrated.
Keep a record of your sightings by checking the boxes.